REALDATA

Data and Exercises
for
Finance and Economics

Robert W. Kolb

and

Brian S. Wilson

Kolb Publishing Company   Miami, Florida

Printed in the United States of America.

Library of Congress Catalog Card Number   92-75394

ISBN: 1-878975-24-2

K Kolb Publishing Company
4705 S.W. 72nd Avenue   Miami, Florida 33155
KOLB (305) 663-0550   FAX (305) 663-6579

Preface

REALDATA: Data and Exercises for Finance and Economics consists of financial and economic data on diskettes accompanied by this text explaining how to access the data and use this information to solve problems in college finance and economics classes. All of the data series are real-world data drawn from a variety of public sources. Many data series, mostly beginning in 1970, are monthly, while others are quarterly.

REALDATA covers both the financial and real sectors of the economy, from T-bills to trade balances, from inflation to business inventories, from the money supply to manufacturing, from foreign exchange to fixed corporate investment, from bonds to the business cycle, from consumer credit to commodity prices. In total, *REALDATA* includes almost 700 time series of actual historical data that many students analyze in class projects and in their own research. All data are contained in a total of 38 spreadsheets for easy access. (The files are Lotus WK1 files and are accessible by all major spreadsheet programs.) All together, *REALDATA* has almost three megabytes of data.

This text is divided into four chapters. The first chapter gives a broad overview of *REALDATA* and explains how to install the data files. Chapter 1 also gives some hints on how to use the spreadsheets to analyze the data accurately and efficiently. Chapters 2 and 3 describe each data series. Chapter 2 provides definitions for all of the financial sector variables, and Chapter 3 defines each variable from the real sector.

Chapter 4 contains more than 100 exercises that can be solved completely using *REALDATA* spreadsheets and any spreadsheet program. These exercises require comparing different variables and drawing inferences about markets and economic trends. Many exercises require the student to complete a graph, while others focus on statistical calculations.

How to Use REALDATA

For almost any class in finance or economics, this text includes a number of exercises directly relevant to the course material. Instructors can assign various exercises just as they are presented in the text. (An Instructor's Manual with complete solutions is available to professors.) All of the exercises can be solved completely with a spreadsheet program.

The data contained in *REALDATA* are extremely rich, and class projects of the instructor's own devising can be built around the data. For example, *REALDATA* includes 60 monthly stock prices and dividend information for 60 different companies, including major industrial companies, small firms, and high-tech firms. Students in an investment course might be assigned projects in portfolio construction using these data. The range of applications for these data is limited only by the imagination and interest of the user.

Future Editions and User Contributions

Assuming interest warrants, we plan to update the spreadsheets frequently. The first printing of *REALDATA* was accompanied by data extending into the second half of 1992.

Ideally, we would like to update the spreadsheets annually. Each exercise included in this text includes an acknowledgment for a contributor. In future editions, we would like to include many more exercises from a diverse authorship. Users of *REALDATA* are invited to contribute new exercises (with detailed solutions please) for future editions. Each exercise that we are able to include will be accompanied by an acknowledgement of the contributor.

Acknowledgments
The firms and institutions listed below granted permission for their proprietary data series to be included in *REALDATA*. The source of each data series is included in the data descriptions of Chapters 2 and 3. To all of these data sources, our profound thanks.

American Stock Exchange
Commodity Research Bureau
Commodity Systems, Inc.
The Conference Board
Fidelity Investments
Frank Russell Associates
Institute of Social Research at the University of Michigan
Lipper Analytical Services
Moody's Investors Service
Morgan Stanley and Company, Inc.
National Association of Securities Dealers
New York Stock Exchange
Salomon Brothers, Inc.
Standard & Poor's Corporation
Wilshire Associates

We would also like to offer special thanks to Ricardo Rodriguez, Andrea Coens, and Joe Rodriguez. Ricardo contributed about 30 exercises to this first edition, Andrea edited the entire manuscript, and Joe designed the cover.

Robert W. Kolb
Brian S. Wilson
University of Miami

Contents

1

Introduction and Installation

What Is *REALDATA?*

REALDATA: Data and Exercises for Finance and Economics provides real-world data in a convenient and consistent format to support the study of finance and economics. *REALDATA* includes almost 700 monthly and quarterly financial and economic time series covering the post World War II period. Chapters 2 and 3 of this text describe these data completely.

All of the data series in *REALDATA* are contained in WK1 format spreadsheets for consistency of presentation and ease of access. All data files can be used by all major spreadsheet products including Lotus 123, Quattro Pro, Excel, and many others. Any program that can read a WK1 format file has full access to *REALDATA* information.

The second half of this book contains more than 100 exercises that can be completed using the data contained in *REALDATA*. The exercises are designed so that they can be solved completely using a typical spreadsheet program. These exercises differ widely in the kinds of activity that they require. Some simply require that the user find certain information in the *REALDATA* files, while others have solutions that result from fairly elaborate computations. Still others call for the creation and interpretation of a graph, and some exercises demand all of these activities.

The remainder of this chapter provides a more detailed overview of *REALDATA*. It explains how to install the *REALDATA* files and discusses the standardized format of the files. The chapter concludes with a discussion of how to solve the exercises using a typical spreadsheet program.

Types of Data in *REALDATA*

Data for the financial sector include information on the Federal Reserve, federal financing, the stock and bond markets, stock market activity and trends, the money markets, the money supply, deposit institution lending, federal credit agencies, finance companies, mortgage markets, the primary market, stock market activity, foreign stock, money, and bond markets, foreign exchange, and inflation in the United States and many other countries. In addition, *REALDATA* offers coverage of individual mutual funds and contains monthly price and dividend information on more than 50 individual stocks. Chapter 2 describes data from the financial sector in detail.

For the real sector, *REALDATA* features data on federal taxation and expenditures, indicators of the business cycle, national income and product accounts, inventories, industrial production, wages and incomes, corporate profits, the automotive, construction, and energy sectors, manufacturing, trade balances between the United States and many other countries, employment, consumer credit, and foreign industrial production and investment. Chapter 3 provides full coverage of real sector data included in *REALDATA*.

Installing *REALDATA* Files

This book is accompanied by two 3.5" 720k distribution diskettes. **The files on the distribution diskettes must be installed before use. These files cannot be read directly.** This section describes the simple steps necessary to install the REALDATA files and prepare them for use. Each *REALDATA* distribution diskette contains its own installation program, which allows installation to a choice of five media or installation targets:

    hard drive
    5.25" 360k diskette
    5.25" 1.2 meg diskette
    3.5" 720k diskette
    3.5" 1.44 meg diskette

To install all of the *REALDATA* files, you will need to have the correct number of blank formatted diskettes of the type that you have chosen as the installation target. Complete installation of all *REALDATA* files from both installation diskettes requires one of the following amounts of space:

    2.6 megabytes of hard disk space
    8 5.25" 360k diskettes
    4 5.25" 1.2 meg diskettes
    4 3.5" 720k diskettes
    2 3.5" 1.44 meg diskettes

Each installation diskette is completely self-contained. Installation to a hard drive is best, because it is much more convenient than installation to a floppy, and access to the data is much faster.

Throughout these instructions, we assume that you plan to install from floppy drive B. The installation process is virtually identical if you wish to install from floppy drive A. If you plan to install from drive A, merely substitute "A" for "B" as the drive designation in the instructions that follow.

1. If you are installing to floppy diskettes, prepare the correct number of formatted diskettes based on the type of diskette you have chosen and the requirements shown above.

2. To start the installation program, place a distribution diskette in floppy drive B.

3. From the DOS prompt, type "B:" and press the ENTER key.

4. Type "INSTALL" and press the ENTER key.

5. The program now asks for your choice of installation target, which can be either to a hard drive or to a floppy drive. Choose a number 1-5 that corresponds to the installation strategy that you have chosen. Alternatively, you may press the escape key (ESC) to terminate the installation.

    A. If you have chosen to install to a hard drive (choice number 1), the installation program now asks you to confirm the installation source and target. The program assumes that you will be installing from the B: floppy drive to C:\REALDATA, meaning hard drive C and directory REALDATA. If that is correct, merely press ENTER. If you wish to install to a different hard drive or path, you can specify the exact name of the target path for the installation. Once the source and target are correct, press function key F1.

    B. If you have chosen to install to a floppy drive (choice numbers 2-5), the installation program now asks you to confirm the installation source and target. The program assumes that you will be installing from floppy drive B to A. If that is correct, merely press function key F1. If you wish to install from or to a different floppy drive, you can specify your chosen source and target floppy drives. Once the source and target are correct, press function key F1.

6. If you have chosen to install to a hard drive, the installation program will now complete the installation for you. If you are installing to floppy diskettes, the installation program will complete the first target diskette and prompt you to place fresh diskettes in the target drive that you have selected.

Following steps 1-6 completes installation of one of the original distribution diskettes. To completely install *REALDATA*, repeat steps 1-6 for the second distribution diskette. After completing the installation, store the *REALDATA* distribution diskettes in a safe place.

REALDATA Spreadsheet Formats and Conventions

All *REALDATA* spreadsheets are organized in a similar manner. The first row of every spreadsheet contains a name that identifies the particular variable. The first column (column A) of each spreadsheet indicates the year of the data, with each row of column A indicating the specific year for all data points on that row. The second column (column B) holds an identifier for either the month or the quarter. Each row of column B holds a number 1–12 if the data in that spreadsheet are monthly data, or it holds a number 1–4 if the data in that spreadsheet are quarterly data. For spreadsheets with monthly data, the number in column B indicates the month of the data, with 1 for January, 2 for February, and so on. For spreadsheets with quarterly data, the number in column B indicates whether the data are for the first, second, third, or fourth quarter. The actual data begin in the third column (column C).

The descriptions of the data in Chapters 2 and 3 give full information about the spreadsheets and the data they contain. As an example, consider Figure 1.1, which is drawn from Chapter 2:

Figure 1.1

Money Supply Measures
Spreadsheet: MONEYSUP.WK1   Monthly Data

A   Year of the observation
    Code: MSYR

B   Month of the observation (1 = January; 2 = February; etc.)
    Code: MSMO

C   M1: Sum of currency, demand deposits, travelers checks and other checkable deposits; averages of daily figures; billions of dollars, seasonally adjusted; from January 1970.
    Source: Board of Governors of the Federal Reserve System, *Statistical Release: Money Stock Measures and Liquid Assets,* H.6, various issues.
    Code: MS001

The heading (Money Supply Measures) indicates the topic area covered by a particular spreadsheet. In general, the spreadsheets are organized topically—they contain data on related variables pertaining to a topic area. The next line gives the name of the spreadsheet. In this example, the spreadsheet is named "MONEYSUP.WK1," and the same line indicates whether the data are monthly or quarterly. For MONEYSUP.WK1, the data are monthly. (A particular spreadsheet holds either monthly data or quarterly data; the two are never mixed.)

Subsequent lines describe the contents of each column in the spreadsheet. As already mentioned, column A indicates the year of the observation, and column B indicates the month or quarter of the year for an observation. For each variable, the first row holds an alphanumeric code or variable identifier. For column A of MONEYSUP.WK1, the code is "MSYR." For columns that hold actual data, like column C in our example, the entry describes the data, indicates the source from which the data are drawn, and specifies the code for the particular variable.

The data description also specifies the first period for which data are available. As the example indicates, column C of MONEYSUP.WK1 holds data on the M1 measure of the money supply and the data begin in January 1970. Some variables have missing values, a problem that plagues all data sources. Throughout the *REALDATA* spreadsheets, missing values are indicated by a value of –99.99.

Solution Techniques and Hints for *REALDATA* Exercises

The exercises in this text typically specify a starting and ending date for the data to be used in the exercise. Follow this specification closely to get the correct answer. Similarly, the exercises that require a graph specify the range for the horizontal and vertical axes. Create your graph using the same axes ranges as specified in the text.

Many exercises require the computation of statistical measures such as the variance or standard deviation of some observations. All solutions to *REALDATA* exercises should use the population measures for the variance and standard deviation, unless your instructor indicates otherwise. For example, the population variance is computed by dividing the sum of squared deviations by the full number of observations. By contrast, sample variances are computed by dividing the sum of square deviations by the number of observations minus one. Most spreadsheets provide functions for computing both the population and sample measures of variances and standard deviations. Generally, the population measures are named "@VAR" and "@STD" for the variance and standard deviation, respectively. The sample measures are typically named "@VARS" and "@STDS." Solutions to *REALDATA* exercises should use the @VAR and @STD functions.

Some exercises ask you to compute the correlation between two variables. Unfortunately, most spreadsheets do not include a correlation function. Nonetheless, correlations can be computed fairly easily by using the spreadsheet's regression feature. To compute a correlation between variables X and Y, follow these steps. First, regress X on Y or regress Y on X. (For our limited purpose, the two are equivalent.) Second, compute the square root of the R^2 provided as part of the regression output. The result is the absolute value of the correlation between variables X and Y. Thus, it still remains to determine whether the correlation is positive or negative, as correlations can be as small as -1.0 or as large as +1.0. Third, the sign of the correlation is the same as the sign of the slope coefficient that is computed as part of the regression.

Most *REALDATA* spreadsheets contain several variables. It is generally easier to solve an exercise if the working spreadsheet is free of extraneous data. To solve a particular exercise, begin by identifying the necessary spreadsheet with the data for the exercise, and copy it to a temporary file, such as TEMP.WK1. Working on spreadsheet TEMP, delete the columns containing variables that are not of interest and delete rows for periods outside the time period of interest. You can then make the computations that the exercise requires. Be sure not to delete portions of the original spreadsheet, or it will be necessary to re-install from the *REALDATA* distribution diskettes.

2
The Financial Sector

Monetary Measures and Federal Finance

Money Supply Measures
Spreadsheet: MONEYSUP.WK1   Monthly Data

A   Year of the observation
    Code: MSYR

B   Month of the observation (1 = January; 2 = February; etc.)
    Code: MSMO

C   M1: Sum of currency, demand deposits, travelers checks, and other checkable deposits; averages of daily figures; billions of dollars; seasonally adjusted; from January 1970.
    Source: Board of Governors of the Federal Reserve System, *Statistical Release: Money Stock Measures and Liquid Assets,* H.6, various issues.
    Code: MS001

D   M2: M1 plus overnight RP's and Eurodollars, MMMF balances, MMDA's, and savings and small time deposits; averages of daily figures; billions of dollars; seasonally adjusted; from January 1970.
Source: Board of Governors of the Federal Reserve System, *Statistical Release: Money Stock Measures and Liquid Assets*, H.6, various issues.
Code: MS002

E   M3: M2 plus large time deposits, term RP's, term Eurodollars, and institution-only MMMF balances; averages of daily figures; billions of dollars; seasonally adjusted; from January 1970.
Source: Board of Governors of the Federal Reserve System, *Statistical Release: Money Stock Measures and Liquid Assets*, H.6, various issues.
Code: MS003

F   L: M3 plus other liquid assets; averages of daily figures; billions of dollars; seasonally adjusted; from January 1970.
Source: Board of Governors of the Federal Reserve System, *Statistical Release: Money Stock Measures and Liquid Assets*, H.6, various issues.
Code: MS004

G   Components of money stock measures and liquid assets: Currency; average of daily figures; billions of dollars; seasonally adjusted; from January 1970.
Source: Board of Governors of the Federal Reserve System, *Statistical Release: Money Stock Measures and Liquid Assets*, H.6, various issues.
Code: MS005

H   Components of money stock measures and liquid assets: Travelers checks; average of daily figures; billions of dollars; seasonally adjusted; from January 1970.
Source: Board of Governors of the Federal Reserve System, *Statistical Release: Money Stock Measures and Liquid Assets*, H.6, various issues.
Code: MS006

I   Components of money stock measures and liquid assets: Demand deposits; average of daily figures; billions of dollars; seasonally adjusted; from January 1970.
Source: Board of Governors of the Federal Reserve System, *Statistical Release: Money Stock Measures and Liquid Assets*, H.6, various issues.
Code: MS007

J Components of money stock measures and liquid assets: Other checkable deposits; average of daily figures; billions of dollars; seasonally adjusted; from January 1970.
Source: Board of Governors of the Federal Reserve System, *Statistical Release: Money Stock Measures and Liquid Assets,* H.6, various issues.
Code: MS008

K Components of money stock measures and liquid assets: Overnight repurchase agreements, general purpose and broker/dealer; average of daily figures; billions of dollars; from January 1970.
Source: Board of Governors of the Federal Reserve System, *Statistical Release: Money Stock Measures and Liquid Assets,* H.6, various issues.
Code: MS009

L Components of money stock measures and liquid assets: Overnight Eurodollars, general purpose and broker/dealer; average of daily figures; billions of dollars; from January 1977.
Source: Board of Governors of the Federal Reserve System, *Statistical Release: Money Stock Measures and Liquid Assets,* H.6, various issues.
Code: MS010

M Components of money stock measures and liquid assets: Money market mutual fund balances, general purpose and broker/dealer; average of daily figures; billions of dollars; from January 1974.
Source: Board of Governors of the Federal Reserve System, *Statistical Release: Money Stock Measures and Liquid Assets,* H.6, various issues.
Code: MS011

N Components of money stock measures and liquid assets: Savings deposits including money market deposit accounts; average of daily figures; billions of dollars; seasonally adjusted; from January 1970.
Source: Board of Governors of the Federal Reserve System, *Statistical Release: Money Stock Measures and Liquid Assets,* H.6, various issues.
Code: MS012

O   Components of money stock measures and liquid assets: Small denomination time deposits (less than $100,000); average of daily figures; billions of dollars; seasonally adjusted; from January 1970.
    Source: Board of Governors of the Federal Reserve System, *Statistical Release: Money Stock Measures and Liquid Assets,* H.6, various issues.
    Code: MS013

P   Components of money stock measures and liquid assets: Large denomination time deposits (greater than $100,000); average of daily figures; billions of dollars; seasonally adjusted; from January 1970.
    Source: Board of Governors of the Federal Reserve System, *Statistical Release: Money Stock Measures and Liquid Assets,* H.6, various issues.
    Code: MS014

Q   Components of money stock measures and liquid assets: Term repurchase agreements at commercial banks; average of daily figures; billions of dollars; from January 1970.
    Source: Board of Governors of the Federal Reserve System, *Statistical Release: Money Stock Measures and Liquid Assets,* H.6, various issues.
    Code: MS015

R   Components of money stock measures and liquid assets: Term repurchase agreements at thrift institutions; average of daily figures; billions of dollars; from January 1971.
    Source: Board of Governors of the Federal Reserve System, *Statistical Release: Money Stock Measures and Liquid Assets,* H.6, various issues.
    Code: MS016

S   Components of money stock measures and liquid assets: Term Eurodollars; average of daily figures; billions of dollars; from January 1970.
    Source: Board of Governors of the Federal Reserve System, *Statistical Release: Money Stock Measures and Liquid Assets,* H.6, various issues.
    Code: MS017

T   Components of money stock measures and liquid assets: Money market mutual fund balances; (institution only); average of daily figures; billions of dollars; from January 1974.

Source: Board of Governors of the Federal Reserve System, *Statistical Release: Money Stock Measures and Liquid Assets,* H.6, various issues.

Code: MS018

U   Components of money stock measures and liquid assets: Bankers' Acceptances; average of daily figures; billions of dollars; seasonally adjusted; from January 1970.

Source: Board of Governors of the Federal Reserve System, *Statistical Release: Money Stock Measures and Liquid Assets,* H.6, various issues.

Code: MS019

V   Components of money stock measures and liquid assets: Commercial paper; average of daily figures; billions of dollars; seasonally adjusted; from January 1970.

Source: Board of Governors of the Federal Reserve System, *Statistical Release: Money Stock Measures and Liquid Assets,* H.6, various issues.

Code: MS020

W   Components of money stock measures and liquid assets: Short-term Treasury securities (held by other than depository institutions, money market mutual funds, and foreign entities) average of daily figures; billions of dollars; seasonally adjusted; from January 1970.

Source: Board of Governors of the Federal Reserve System, *Statistical Release: Money Stock Measures and Liquid Assets,* H.6, various issues.

Code: MS021

Depository Institution Reserves
Spreadsheet: RESERVES.WK1   Monthly Data

A   Year of the observation
     Code: RESYR

B   Month of the observation (1 = January; 2 = February; etc.)
     Code: RESMO

C   Reserves of Depository Institutions: Total; adjusted for changes in reserve requirements; average of daily figures; millions of dollars; seasonally adjusted; from January 1970.
     Source: *Federal Reserve Bulletin*, Table 1.20, various issues.
     Code: RES001

D   Reserves of Depository Institutions: Nonborrowed; adjusted for changes in reserve requirements; average of daily figures; millions of dollars; seasonally adjusted; from January 1970.
     Source: *Federal Reserve Bulletin*, Table 1.20, various issues.
     Code: RES002

E   Reserves of Depository Institutions: Nonborrowed plus extended credit; adjusted for changes in reserve requirements; average of daily figures; millions of dollars; seasonally adjusted; from January 1970.
     Source: *Federal Reserve Bulletin*, Table 1.20, various issues.
     Code: RES003

F   Reserves of Depository Institutions: Required; adjusted for changes in reserve requirements; average of daily figures; millions of dollars; seasonally adjusted; from January 1970.
     Source: *Federal Reserve Bulletin*, Table 1.20, various issues.
     Code: RES004

G   Reserves of Depository Institutions: Excess; average of daily figures; millions of dollars; from January 1970.
     Source: *Federal Reserve Bulletin*, Table 1.20, various issues.
     Code: RES005

H   Monetary Base: Adjusted for changes in reserve requirements; average daily figures; millions of dollars; seasonally adjusted; from January 1970.
     Source: *Federal Reserve Bulletin*, Table 1.20, various issues.
     Code: RES006

I   Total Vault Cash: Average daily figures; millions of dollars; from January 1970.
      Source: *Federal Reserve Bulletin*, Table 1.20, various issues.
      Code: RES007

Federal Credit Agencies
Spreadsheet: FEDCRED.WK1   Monthly Data

A   Year of the observation
      Code: FCYR

B   Month of the observation (1 = January; 2 = February; etc.)
      Code: FCMO

C   Debt of Federal and Federally Sponsored Agencies: Total; millions of dollars; from January 1970.
      Source: *Federal Reserve Bulletin*, Table 1.44; various issues.
      Code: FC001

D   Debt of Federal Agencies: Government National Mortgage Association certificates of participation; millions of dollars; from January 1970.
      Source: *Federal Reserve Bulletin*, Table 1.44; various issues.
      Code: FC002

E   Debt of Federally Sponsored Agencies: Federal Home Loan Mortgage Corporation; millions of dollars; from January 1970.
      Source: *Federal Reserve Bulletin*, Table 1.44; various issues.
      Code: FC003

F   Debt of Federally Sponsored Agencies: Federal National Mortgage Association; millions of dollars; from January 1970.
      Source: *Federal Reserve Bulletin*, Table 1.44; various issues.
      Code: FC004

Inflation
Spreadsheet: INFLATE.WK1   Monthly Data

A   Year of the observation
     Code: INFYR

B   Month of the observation (1 = January; 2 = February; etc.)
     Code: INFMO

C   Consumer Price Index: All Items, (1982-84=100) seasonally adjusted; from
     January 1970.
     Source: U.S. Department of Labor, Bureau of Labor Statistics, *The Consumer*
     Price Index, various issues.
     Code: INF001

D   Consumer Price Index: Food and Beverages, (1982-84=100) seasonally
     adjusted; from January 1970.
     Source: U.S. Department of Labor, Bureau of Labor Statistics, *The Consumer*
     Price Index, various issues.
     Code: INF002

E   Consumer Price Index: Housing, (1982-84=100) seasonally adjusted; from
     January 1970.
     Source: U.S. Department of Labor, Bureau of Labor Statistics, *The Consumer*
     Price Index, various issues.
     Code: INF003

F   Consumer Price Index: Commodities, (1982-84=100) seasonally adjusted; from
     January 1970.
     Source: U.S. Department of Labor, Bureau of Labor Statistics, *The Consumer*
     Price Index, various issues.
     Code: INF004

G   Consumer Price Index: Services, (1982-84=100) seasonally adjusted; from
     January 1970.
     Source: U.S. Department of Labor, Bureau of Labor Statistics, *The Consumer*
     Price Index, various issues.
     Code: INF005

H   Producer Price Index: Finished Goods, (1982-84=100) seasonally adjusted; from
     January 1970.
     Source: U.S. Department of Labor, Bureau of Labor Statistics, *The Producer*
     Price Index, various issues.
     Code: INF006

I   Producer Price Index: Intermediate Materials, Supplies, & Components (1982-84=100) seasonally adjusted; from January 1970.
     Source: U.S. Department of Labor, Bureau of Labor Statistics, *The Producer Price Index*, various issues.
     Code: INF007

J   Producer Price Index: Crude Materials for Further Processing (1982-84=100) seasonally adjusted; from January 1970.
     Source: U.S. Department of Labor, Bureau of Labor Statistics, *The Producer Price Index*, various issues.
     Code: INF008

K   Producer Price Index: All Commodities (1982-84=100); from January 1970.
     Source: U.S. Department of Labor, Bureau of Labor Statistics, *The Producer Price Index*, various issues.
     Code: INF009

L   Producer Price Index: Farm Products, Processed Foods, and Feeds (1982-84=100); from January 1970.
     Source: U.S. Department of Labor, Bureau of Labor Statistics, *The Producer Price Index*, various issues.
     Code: INF010

M   Producer Price Index: Industrial Commodities (1982-84=100); from January 1970.
     Source: U.S. Department of Labor, Bureau of Labor Statistics, *The Producer Price Index*, various issues.
     Code: INF011

N   Consumer Price Indexes (1982-84=100); United States; from January 1970.
     Source: *Survey of Current Business*, various issues.
     Code: INF012

Foreign Inflation
Spreadsheet: FORINFLA.WK1   Monthly Data

A   Year of the observation
    Code: FINFYR

B   Month of the observation (1 = January; 2 = February; etc.)
    Code: FINFMO

C   Consumer Price Indexes (1982-84=100); United States; from January 1970.
    Source: *Survey of Current Business*, various issues.
    Code: FINF001

D   Consumer Price Indexes (1982-84=100); Japan; from January 1970.
    Source: *Survey of Current Business*, Table 15, various issues.
    Code: FINF002

E   Consumer Price Indexes (1982-84=100); Federal Republic of Germany; from
    January 1970.
    Source: *Survey of Current Business*, Table 15, various issues.
    Code: FINF003

F   Consumer Price Indexes (1982-84=100); France; from January 1970.
    Source: *Survey of Current Business*, Table 15, various issues.
    Code: FINF004

G   Consumer Price Indexes (1982-84=100); United Kingdom; from January 1970.
    Source: *Survey of Current Business*, Table 15, various issues.
    Code: FINF005

H   Consumer Price Indexes (1982-84=100); Italy; from January 1970.
    Source: *Survey of Current Business*, Table 15, various issues.
    Code: FINF006

I   Consumer Price Indexes (1982-84=100); Canada; from January 1970.
    Source: *Survey of Current Business*, Table 15, various issues.
    Code: FINF007

Financial Institutions

Depository Institutions
Spreadsheet: DEPOSINS.WK1   Monthly Data

A   Year of the observation
     Code: DEPYR

B   Month of the observation (1 = January; 2 = February; etc.)
     Code: DEPMO

C   Loans and Securities at all Commercial Banks: Total; billions of dollars; seasonally adjusted; from January 1973.
     Source: *Federal Reserve Bulletin,* Table 1.23, various issues.
     Code: DEP001

D   Loans and Securities at all Commercial Banks: U.S. government securities; billions of dollars; seasonally adjusted; from January 1973.
     Source: *Federal Reserve Bulletin,* Table 1.23, various issues.
     Code: DEP002

E   Loans and Securities at all Commercial Banks: Total loans and leases; billions of dollars; seasonally adjusted; from January 1973.
     Source: *Federal Reserve Bulletin,* Table 1.23, various issues.
     Code: DEP003

F   Loans and Securities at all Commercial Banks: Commercial and industrial loans outstanding plus nonfinancial commercial paper; seasonally adjusted; millions of dollars; from January 1970.
     Source: *Survey of Current Business,* various issues.
     Code: DEP004

G   Assets and Liabilities of Commercial Banks: Loans and investments excluding interbank: millions of dollars; from January 1980.
     Source: *Federal Reserve Bulletin,* various issues.
     Code: DEP005

H   Assets and Liabilities of Commercial Banks: Total cash assets; millions of dollars; from January 1980.
     Source: *Federal Reserve Bulletin,* various issues.
     Code: DEP006

I   Assets and Liabilities of Commercial Banks: Other assets (1980-1983 series include Interbank loans); total: millions of dollars; from January 1980.
     Source: *Federal Reserve Bulletin,* various issues.
     Code: DEP007

J   Assets and Liabilities of Commercial Banks: Total deposits; millions of dollars; from January 1980.
     Source: *Federal Reserve Bulletin,* various issues.
     Code: DEP008

K   Assets and Liabilities of Commercial Banks: Transaction accounts (1980-1983 series listed as Demand Accounts); total; millions of dollars; from January 1980.
     Source: *Federal Reserve Bulletin,* various issues.
     Code: DEP009

L   Assets and Liabilities of Commercial Banks: Savings deposits; millions of dollars; from January 1980.
     Source: *Federal Reserve Bulletin,* various issues.
     Code: DEP010

M   Assets and Liabilities of Commercial Banks: Time deposits; millions of dollars; from January 1980.
     Source: *Federal Reserve Bulletin,* various issues.
     Code: DEP011

N   Savings Institutions (SAIF Insured Institutions): Total assets; millions of dollars; from January 1976.
     Source: *Federal Reserve Bulletin,* Table 1.37 various issues.
     Code: DEP012

O   Savings Institutions (SAIF Insured Institutions): Mortgages and mortgage securities outstanding; net total; millions of dollars; from January 1976.
     Source: *Federal Reserve Bulletin,* Table 1.37 various issues.
     Code: DEP013

P   Savings Institutions (SAIF Insured Institutions): Nonmortgage loans outstanding, consumer; end of month; millions of dollars; from January 1970.
     Source: *Federal Reserve Bulletin,* Table 1.37, various issues.
     Code: DEP014

Q   Savings Institutions (SAIF Insured Institutions): Nonmortgage loans outstanding; commercial; end of month; millions of dollars; from January 1976.
Source: *Federal Reserve Bulletin*, Table 1.37, various issues.
Code: DEP015

R   Savings Institutions (SAIF Insured Institutions): Borrowings; total; end of month; millions of dollars; from January 1976.
Source: *Federal Reserve Bulletin*, Table 1.37, various issues.
Code: DEP016

Consumer Credit
Spreadsheet: CONSUMCR.WK1   Monthly Data

A   Year of the observation
Code: CCRYR

B   Month of the observation (1 = January; 2 = February; etc.)
Code: CCRMO

C   Consumer Installment Credit Outstanding; total; seasonally adjusted; millions of dollars; from January 1975.
Source: American Bankers Association, Installment Credit Committee, *Delinquency Rates on Bank Installment Loans*, various issues.
Code: CCR001

D   Consumer Installment Credit Outstanding; total; Commercial Banks; millions of dollars; seasonally adjusted; from January 1970.
Source: American Bankers Association, Installment Credit Committee, *Delinquency Rates on Bank Installment Loans*, various issues.
Code: CCR002

E   Consumer Installment Credit Outstanding; automobile; millions of dollars; seasonally adjusted; from January 1975.
Source: American Bankers Association, Installment Credit Committee, *Delinquency Rates on Bank Installment Loans*, various issues.
Code: CCR003

F   Consumer Installment Credit Outstanding; revolving; millions of dollars; seasonally adjusted; from January 1980.
Source: American Bankers Association, Installment Credit Committee, *Delinquency Rates on Bank Installment Loans*, various issues.
Code: CCR004

G   Consumer Installment Credit Outstanding; revolving; commercial banks; millions of dollars; seasonally adjusted; from January 1970.
Source: American Bankers Association, Installment Credit Committee, *D*
Code: CCR005

H   Consumer Installment Credit Outstanding; revolving; retailers; millions of dollars; seasonally adjusted; from January 1977.
Source: American Bankers Association, Installment Credit Committee, *D*
Code: CCR006

I   Consumer Installment Credit Outstanding; revolving; gasoline companies; millions of dollars; seasonally adjusted; from January 1971.
Source: American Bankers Association, Installment Credit Committee, *D*
Code: CCR007

J   Consumer Installment Credit Outstanding; mobile homes; millions of dollars; seasonally adjusted; from January 1975.
Source: American Bankers Association, Installment Credit Committee, *D*
Code: CCR008

Mutual Funds Indexes
Spreadsheet: LIPPER.WK1   Monthly Data

A   Year of the observation
Code: LIPYR

B   Month of the observation (1 = January; 2 = February; etc.)
Code: LIPMO

C   Lipper Mutual Fund Index: Capital Appreciation; net asset value weighted index of the 30 largest Capital Appreciation funds; adjusted for dividends and capital gains distributions as of the ex-dividend dates; December 31, 1980=100; from December 1986.
Source: Lipper Analytical Services.
Code: LIP001

D   Lipper Mutual Fund Index: Balanced; net asset value weighted index of the 30 largest funds within the Balanced Fund investment objective; adjusted for income dividends and capital gains distributions as of the ex-dividend dates; December 31, 1960=100; from December 1986.
Source: Lipper Analytical Services.
Code: LIP002

E   Lipper Mutual Fund Index: Equity Income; net asset value weighted index of the 30 largest Equity Income mutual funds; adjusted for income dividends and capital gains distributions as of the ex-dividend dates; December 31, 1978=100; from January 1990.
Source: Lipper Analytical Services.
Code: LIP003

F   Lipper Mutual Fund Index: Gold; net asset value weighted index of the 10 largest funds within the Gold fund category; adjusted for income dividends and capital gains distributions as of the ex-dividend dates; December 31, 1984=100; from December 1986.
Source: Lipper Analytical Services.
Code: LIP004

G   Lipper Mutual Fund Index: Growth; net asset value weighted index of the 30 largest Growth mutual funds; adjusted for income dividends and capital gains distributions as of the ex-dividend dates; December 31, 1968=100; from December 1986.
Source: Lipper Analytical Services.
Code: LIP005

H   Lipper Mutual Fund Index: Growth and Income; net asset value weighted index of the 30 largest funds within the Growth and Income objective; adjusted for income dividends and capital gains distributions as of the ex-dividend dates; December 31, 1968=100; from December 1986.
Source: Lipper Analytical Services.
Code: LIP006

I   Lipper Mutual Fund Index: International; net asset value weighted index of the 30 largest funds within the International Funds category; adjusted for income dividends and capital gains distributions as of the ex-dividend dates; December 31, 1968=100; from December 1984.
Source: Lipper Analytical Services.
Code: LIP007

J   Lipper Mutual Fund Index: Science & Technology; net asset value weighted index of the 10 largest funds within the Science & Technology investment objective; adjusted for income dividends and capital gains distributions as of the ex-dividend dates; December 31, 1984=100; from December 1984.
Source: Lipper Analytical Services.
Code: LIP008

K   Lipper Mutual Fund Index: Small Company Growth; net asset value weighted index of the 30 largest Small Company Growth funds; adjusted for income dividends and capital gains distributions as of the ex-dividend dates; December 31, 1980=100; from December 1984.
Source: Lipper Analytical Services.
Code: LIP009

Individual Mutual Funds
Spreadsheet: MUTUFUND.WK1   Monthly Data

A   Year of the observation
Code: INMFYR

B   Month of the observation (1 = January; 2 = February; etc.)
Code: INMFMO

C   Mutual Fund Net Asset Values: Fidelity Funds: Capital Appreciation Fund; end of month closing; from January 1987.
Source: Fidelity Investments.
Code: INMF001P

D   Mutual Fund Dividends: Fidelity Funds: Capital Appreciation Fund; from January 1987.
Source: Fidelity Investments.
Code: INMF001D

E   Mutual Fund Net Asset Values: Fidelity Funds: Global Bond Fund; end of month closing; from April 1989.
Source: Fidelity Investments.
Code: INMF002P

F   Mutual Fund Dividends: Fidelity Funds: Global Bond Fund; from April 1989.
Source: Fidelity Investments.
Code: INMF002D

G   Mutual Fund Net Asset Values: Fidelity Funds: Growth and Income Fund; end of month closing; from January 1987.
Source: Fidelity Investments.
Code: INMF003P

H   Mutual Fund Dividends: Fidelity Funds: Growth and Income; from January 1987.
Source: Fidelity Investments.
Code: INMF003D

I   Mutual Fund Net Asset Values: Fidelity Funds: High Yield Fund; end of month closing; from December 1986.
Source: Fidelity Investments.
Code: INMF004P

J   Mutual Fund Dividends: Fidelity Funds: High Yield Fund; from December 1986.
    Source: Fidelity Investments.
    Code: INMF004D

K   Mutual Fund Net Asset Values: Fidelity Funds: Magellan Fund; end of month closing; from January 1986.
    Source: Fidelity Investments.
    Code: INMF005P

L   Mutual Fund Dividends: Fidelity Funds: Magellan Fund; from December 1986.
    Source: Fidelity Investments.
    Code: INMF005D

M   Mutual Fund Net Asset Values: Fidelity Funds: Municipal Bond Fund; end of month closing; from December 1986.
    Source: Fidelity Investments.
    Code: INMF006P

N   Mutual Fund Dividends: Fidelity Funds: Municipal Bond Fund; from December 1986.
    Source: Fidelity Investments.
    Code: INMF006D

O   Mutual Fund Net Asset Values: Fidelity Funds: Mortgage Security Fund; end of month closing; from March 1991.
    Source: Fidelity Investments.
    Code: INMF007P

P   Mutual Fund Dividends: Fidelity Funds: Mortgage Security Fund; from March 1991.
    Source: Fidelity Investments.
    Code: INMF007D

Q   Mutual Fund Net Asset Values: Fidelity Funds: Puritan Fund; end of month closing; from January 1987.
    Source: Fidelity Investments.
    Code: INMF008P

R   Mutual Fund Dividends: Fidelity Funds: Puritan Fund; from January 1987.
    Source: Fidelity Investments.
    Code: INMF008D

Financial Markets

The Primary Market
Spreadsheet: PRIMMKT.WK1   Monthly Data

A   Year of the observation
     Code: PMKTYR

B   Month of the observation (1 = January; 2 = February; etc.)
     Code: PMKTMO

C   New Security Issues; U.S. Corporations; all issues; millions of dollars; from January 1970.
     Source: *Federal Reserve Bulletin*, Table 1.46, various issues.
     Code: PMKT001

D   New Security Issues; U.S. Corporations; stocks: (only public offerings); millions of dollars; from January 1977.
     Source: *Federal Reserve Bulletin*, Table 1.46, various issues.
     Code: PMKT002

E   New Security Issues; U.S. Corporations; Stocks: by type of offering: Public preferred; millions of dollars; from January 1977.
     Source: *Federal Reserve Bulletin*, Table 1.46, various issues.
     Code: PMKT003

F   New Security Issues; U.S. Corporations; Stocks: by type of offering: Common; millions of dollars; from January 1970.
     Source: *Federal Reserve Bulletin*, Table 1.46, various issues.
     Code: PMKT004

G   New Security Issues; Tax-Exempt State and Local Governments; General Obligation; millions of dollars; from January 1970.
     Source: *Federal Reserve Bulletin*, Table 1.45, various issues.
     Code: PMKT005

H   New Security Issues; Tax-Exempt State and Local Governments; Revenue; millions of dollars; from January 1970.
     Source: *Federal Reserve Bulletin*, Table 1.45, various issues.
     Code: PMKT006

I   New Security Issues; U.S. Corporations; Bonds; millions of dollars; from January 1970.
     Source: *Federal Reserve Bulletin*, Table 1.46, various issues.
     Code: PMKT007

J   New Security Issues; U.S. Corporations; Bonds: by type of offering: Public; domestic; millions of dollars; from January 1970.
Source: *Federal Reserve Bulletin*, Table 1.46, various issues.
Code: PMKT008

K   New Security Issues; U.S. Corporations; Bonds: by type of offering: Sold abroad; millions of dollars; from January 1983.
Source: *Federal Reserve Bulletin*, Table 1.46, various issues.
Code: PMKT009

Stock Market Prices and Yields
Spreadsheet: STKINDEX.WK1   Monthly Data

A   Year of the observation
Code: STKINYR

B   Month of the observation (1 = January; 2 = February; etc.)
Code: STKINMO

C   Common Stock Prices: Dow Jones 30 Industrial Stocks; Average of Daily Closing Prices; from January 1970.
Source: Dow Jones & Company, *The Wall Street Journal*, various issues.
Code: STKIN001

D   Common Stock Prices: New York Stock Exchange: Composite (1965=50); monthly averages of daily closing rates; from January 1970.
Source: *Federal Reserve Bulletin*, Table 1.36, various issues.
Code: STKIN002

E   Common Stock Prices: New York Stock Exchange: Industrial (1965=50); monthly averages of daily closing rates; from January 1970.
Source: *Federal Reserve Bulletin*, Table 1.36, various issues.
Code: STKIN003

F   Common Stock Prices: New York Stock Exchange: Transportation (1965=50); monthly averages of daily closing rates; from January 1970.
Source: *Federal Reserve Bulletin*, Table 1.36, various issues.
Code: STKIN004

G   Common Stock Prices: New York Stock Exchange: Utility (1965=50); monthly averages of daily closing rates; from January 1970.
Source: *Federal Reserve Bulletin*, Table 1.36, various issues.
Code: STKIN005

H   Common Stock Prices: New York Stock Exchange: Finance (1965=50); monthly averages of daily closing rates; from January 1970.
Source: *Federal Reserve Bulletin,* Table 1.36, various issues.
Code: STKIN006

I   Common Stock Prices: Standard and Poor's Corporation: Composite (S&P's 500) 1941-43=10: monthly average of daily prices; from January 1970.
Source: Standard and Poor's Corporation, *The Outlook,* various issues.
Code: STKIN007

J   Common Stock Prices: Standard and Poor's Corporation: Industrial, 1941-43=10: monthly average of daily prices; from January 1970.
Source: Standard and Poor's Corporation, *The Outlook,* various issues.
Code: STKIN008

K   Common Stock Prices: Standard and Poor's Corporation: Capital Goods, 1941-43=10: monthly average of daily prices; from January 1970.
Source: Standard and Poor's Corporation, *The Outlook,* various issues.
Code: STKIN009

L   Common Stock Prices: Standard and Poor's Corporation: Transportation, 1970=10: monthly average of daily prices; from January 1970.
Source: Standard and Poor's Corporation, *The Outlook,* various issues.
Code: STKIN010

M   Common Stock Prices: Standard and Poor's Corporation: Public Utilities, 1941-43=10: monthly average of daily prices; from January 1970.
Source: Standard and Poor's Corporation, *The Outlook,* various issues.
Code: STKIN011

N   Common Stock Prices: Standard and Poor's Corporation: Finance, 1970=10: monthly average of daily prices; from January 1970.
Source: Standard and Poor's Corporation, *The Outlook,* various issues.
Code: STKIN012

O   NASDAQ over-the-counter price indexes: Composite (2/5/71=100); from January 1971.
Source: *Survey of Current Business,* Table 6 of Current Business Statistics, various issues.
Code: STKIN013

P   NASDAQ over-the-counter price indexes: industrial (2/5/71=100); from January 1971.
     Source: *Survey of Current Business*, Table 6 of Current Business Statistics, various issues.
     Code: STKIN014

Q   NASDAQ over-the-counter price indexes: insurance (2/5/71=100); from January 1971.
     Source: *Survey of Current Business*, Table 6 of Current Business Statistics, various issues.
     Code: STKIN015

R   NASDAQ over-the-counter price indexes: bank (2/5/71=100); from January 1971.
     Source: *Survey of Current Business*, Table 6 of Current Business Statistics, various issues.
     Code: STKIN016

S   Common Stock Prices: Wilshire Associates, Wilshire 5000 Stock Index, from October 1990.
     Source: Commodity Services, Inc.
     Code: STKIN017

T   Common Stock Prices: Frank Russel Corporation, Russell 2000 Stock Index, from January 1979.
     Source: Frank Russell Corporation.
     Code: STKIN018

U   Yields (Standard and Poor's Corp.), percent: composite (500 stocks); from January 1977.
     Source: *Survey of Current Business*, Table 6 of Current Business Statistics, various issues.
     Code: STKIN019

V   Yields (Standard and Poor's Corp.), percent: industrials (400 stocks); from January 1977.
     Source: *Survey of Current Business*, Table 6 of Current Business Statistics, various issues.
     Code: STKIN020

W   Yields (Standard and Poor's Corp.), percent: utilities (40 stocks); from January 1977.
     Source: *Survey of Current Business*, Table 6 of Current Business Statistics, various issues.
     Code: STKIN021

X   Yields (Standard and Poor's Corp.), percent: transportation (20 stocks); from January 1977.
Source: *Survey of Current Business*, Table 6 of Current Business Statistics, various issues.
Code: STKIN022

Y   Yields (Standard and Poor's Corp.), percent: financial (40 stocks); from January 1977.
Source: *Survey of Current Business*, Table 6 of Current Business Statistics, various issues.
Code: STKIN023

Z   Yields (Standard and Poor's Corp.), percent: preferred (10 stocks, high-grade); from January 1977.
Source: *Survey of Current Business*, Table 6 of Current Business Statistics, various issues.
Code: STKIN024

AA   Dividend Yield: Standard and Poor's Common Stock Composite; monthly; percent per annum; from January 1970.
Source: Standard and Poor's Corporation, *The Outlook*, various issues.
Code: STKIN025

AB   Dividend Yield: Standard and Poor's Preferred Stock Yield; monthly; percent per annum; from January 1970.
Source: Standard and Poor's Corporation, *The Outlook*, various issues.
Code: STKIN026

AC   Common Stock Prices: NASDAQ 100 Index; from December 1986.
Source: Commodity Systems, Inc.
Code: STKIN027

AD   Common Stock Prices: Chicago Board Options Exchange 100 Index; from August 1988.
Source: Commodity Systems, Inc.
Code: STKIN028

AE   Common Stock Prices: Major Market Index; Chicago Board of Trade; from December 1986.
Source: Commodity Systems, Inc.
Code: STKIN029

Stock Market Activity
Spreadsheet: STKACTIV.WK1   Monthly Data

A   Year of the observation
Code: STKACYR

B   Month of the observation (1 = January; 2 = February; etc.)
Code: STKACMO

C   Sales: Total on all registered exchanges (SEC); market value; millions of dollars; from January 1977.
Source: *Survey of Current Business*, Table 6 of Current Business Statistics, various issues.
Code: STKAC001

D   Sales: Total on all registered exchanges (SEC); shares sold; millions; from January 1977.
Source: *Survey of Current Business*, Table 6 of Current Business Statistics, various issues.
Code: STKAC002

E   Sales: Total on New York Stock Exchange; market value; millions of dollars; from January 1977.
Source: *Survey of Current Business*, Table 6 of Current Business Statistics, various issues.
Code: STKAC003

F   Sales: Total on New York Stock Exchange; shares sold; (cleared or settled) millions; from January 1977.
Source: *Survey of Current Business*, Table 6 of Current Business Statistics, various issues.
Code: STKAC004

G   Sales: Total on NASDAQ over-the-counter; market value; millions of dollars; from January 1983.
Source: *Survey of Current Business*, Table 6 of Current Business Statistics, various issues.
Code: STKAC005

H   Sales: Total on NASDAQ over-the-counter; shares sold; millions; from November 1971.
Source: *Survey of Current Business*, Table 6 of Current Business Statistics, various issues.
Code: STKAC006

I   Volume Traded on the New York Stock Exchange; millions of shares; monthly average; from January 1970.
     Source: New York Stock Exchange.
     Code: STKAC007

J   Stock Market Composition; reported share volume by size; (at 5000 shares and over); monthly; percent; from January 1970.
     Source: New York Stock Exchange; *Statistical Highlights,* various issues.
     Code: STKAC008

K   Stock Market: Customers' Stock Margin Debt; millions of dollars; from May 1970.
     Source: New York Stock Exchange, *Statistical Highlights,* various issues.
     Code: STKAC009

International Stock Indexes
Spreadsheet: FORSTOCK.WK1   Monthly Data

A   Year of the observation
     Code: FSTKYR

B   Month of the observation (1 = January; 2 = February; etc.)
     Code: FSTKMO

C   Stock Price Indexes (1967=100); United States; from January 1970.
     Source: *Survey of Current Business,* Table 15 of Current Business Statistics, various issues.
     Code: FSTK001

D   Stock Price Indexes (1967=100); Japan; from January 1970.
     Source: *Survey of Current Business,* Table 15 of Current Business Statistics, various issues.
     Code: FSTK002

E   Stock Price Indexes (1967=100); Federal Republic of Germany; from January 1970.
     Source: *Survey of Current Business,* Table 15 of Current Business Statistics, various issues.
     Code: FSTK003

F   Stock Price Indexes (1967=100); France; from January 1970.
     Source: *Survey of Current Business*, Table 15 of Current Business Statistics, various issues.
     Code: FSTK004

G   Stock Price Indexes (1967=100); United Kingdom; from January 1970.
     Source: *Survey of Current Business*, Table 15 of Current Business Statistics, various issues.
     Code: FSTK005

H   Stock Price Indexes (1967=100); Italy; from January 1970.
     Source: *Survey of Current Business*, Table 15 of Current Business Statistics, various issues.
     Code: FSTK006

I   Stock Price Indexes (1967=100); Canada; from January 1970.
     Source: *Survey of Current Business*, Table 15 of Current Business Statistics, various issues.
     Code: FSTK007

J   Stock Price Indexes (December; 1969=100); Europe, Asia, Far East, (EAFE); from January 1970.
     Source: Morgan Stanley and Company, Inc.
     Code: FSTK008

Individual Stock Data
Spreadsheet: STOCKS.WK1   Monthly Data

A   Year of the observation
     Code: STOCKYR

B   Month of the observation (1 = January; 2 = February; etc.)
     Code: STOCKMO

C   Common Stock Prices: Aluminum Co. of America; symbol: AA; exchange: New York Stock Exchange; end of month closing price; adjusted for stock splits; from December 1986.
     Source: Commodity Systems, Inc.
     Code: STOCK001P

D   Common Stock Dividends: Aluminum Co. of America; symbol: AA; exchange: New York Stock Exchange; from December 1986.
     Source: Commodity Systems, Inc.
     Code: STOCK001D

E   Common Stock Prices: Apple Computer; symbol: AAPL; exchange: NASDAQ; end of month closing price; adjusted for stock splits; from December 1986.
Source: Commodity Systems, Inc.
Code: STOCK002P

F   Common Stock Dividends: Apple Computer; symbol: AAPL; exchange: NASDAQ, from December 1986.
Source: Commodity Systems, Inc.
Code: STOCK002D

G   Common Stock Prices: Allied Signal Company; symbol: ALD; exchange: New York Stock Exchange; end of month closing price; adjusted for stock splits; from December 1986.
Source: Commodity Systems, Inc.
Code: STOCK003P

H   Common Stock Dividends: Allied Signal Company; symbol: ALD; exchange: New York Stock Exchange; from December 1986.
Source: Commodity Systems, Inc.
Code: STOCK003D

I   Common Stock Prices: Amgen; symbol: AMGN; exchange: NASDAQ; end of month closing price; adjusted for stock splits; from December 1987.
Source: Commodity Systems, Inc.
Code: STOCK004P

J   Common Stock Dividends: Amgen; symbol: AMGN; exchange: NASDAQ; from December 1987.
Source: Commodity Systems, Inc.
Code: STOCK004D

K   Common Stock Prices: American Express; symbol: AXP; exchange: New York Stock Exchange; end of month closing price; adjusted for stock splits; from December 1986.
Source: Commodity Systems, Inc.
Code: STOCK005P

L   Common Stock Dividends: American Express; symbol: AXP; exchange: New York Stock Exchange; from December 1986.
Source: Commodity Systems, Inc.
Code: STOCK005D

M   Common Stock Prices: The Boeing Co.; symbol: BA; exchange: New York Stock Exchange; end of month closing price; adjusted for stock splits; from December 1986.
Source: Commodity Systems, Inc.
Code: STOCK006P

N   Common Stock Dividends: The Boeing Co.; symbol: BA; exchange: New York Stock Exchange; from December 1986.
Source: Commodity Systems, Inc.
Code: STOCK006D

O   Common Stock Prices: Bethlehem Steel Company; symbol: BS; exchange: New York Stock Exchange; end of month closing price; adjusted for stock splits; from December 1986.
Source: Commodity Systems, Inc.
Code: STOCK007P

P   Common Stock Dividends: Bethlehem Steel Co.; symbol: BS; exchange: New York Stock Exchange; from December 1986.
Source: Commodity Systems, Inc.
Code: STOCK007D

Q   Common Stock Prices: Anheuser Busch Co. ; symbol: BUD; exchange: New York Stock Exchange; end of month closing price; adjusted for stock splits; from December 1986.
Source: Commodity Systems, Inc.
Code: STOCK008P

R   Common Stock Dividends: Anheuser Busch Co.; symbol: BUD; exchange: New York Stock Exchange; from December 1986.
Source: Commodity Systems, Inc.
Code: STOCK008D

S   Common Stock Prices: Caterpillar Tractor; symbol: CAT; exchange: New York Stock Exchange; end of month closing price; adjusted for stock splits; from December 1986.
Source: Commodity Systems, Inc.
Code: STOCK009P

T   Common Stock Dividends: Caterpillar Tractor; symbol: CAT; exchange: New York Stock Exchange; from December 1986.
Source: Commodity Systems, Inc.
Code: STOCK009D

U   Common Stock Prices: Citicorp; symbol: CC; exchange: New York Stock Exchange; end of month closing price; adjusted for stock splits; from December 1986.
Source: Commodity Systems, Inc.
Code: STOCK010P

V   Common Stock Dividends: Citicorp; symbol: CC; exchange: New York Stock Exchange; from December 1986.
Source: Commodity Systems, Inc.
Code: STOCK010D

W   Common Stock Prices: Chevron; symbol: CHV; exchange: New York Stock Exchange; end of month closing price; adjusted for stock splits; from December 1986.
Source: Commodity Systems, Inc.
Code: STOCK011P

X   Common Stock Dividends: Chevron; symbol: CHV; exchange: New York Stock Exchange; from December 1986.
Source: Commodity Systems, Inc.
Code: STOCK011D

Y   Common Stock Prices: Centocor, Inc.; symbol: CNTO; exchange: NASDAQ; end of month closing price; adjusted for stock splits; from March 1990.
Source: Commodity Systems, Inc.
Code: STOCK012P

Z   Common Stock Dividends: Centocor, Inc.; symbol: CNTO; exchange: NASDAQ; from March 1990.
Source: Commodity Systems, Inc.
Code: STOCK012D

AA   Common Stock Prices: Du Pont (El) de Nemour; symbol: DD; exchange: New York Stock Exchange; end of month closing price; adjusted for stock splits; from December 1986.
Source: Commodity Systems, Inc.
Code: STOCK013P

AB   Common Stock Dividends: Du Pont (El) de Nemour; symbol: DD; exchange: New York Stock Exchange; from December 1986.
Source: Commodity Systems, Inc.
Code: STOCK013D

AC Common Stock Prices: Walt Disney Productions; symbol: DIS; exchange: New York Stock Exchange; end of month closing price; adjusted for stock splits; from December 1986.
Source: Commodity Systems, Inc.
Code: STOCK014P

AD Common Stock Dividends: Walt Disney Productions; symbol: DIS; exchange: New York Stock Exchange; from December 1986.
Source: Commodity Systems, Inc.
Code: STOCK014D

AE Common Stock Prices: Dow Chemical Co.; symbol: DOW; exchange: New York Stock Exchange; end of month closing price; adjusted for stock splits; from December 1986.
Source: Commodity Systems, Inc.
Code: STOCK015P

AF Common Stock Dividends: Dow Chemical Co.; symbol: DOW; exchange: New York Stock Exchange; from December 1986.
Source: Commodity Systems, Inc.
Code: STOCK015D

AG Common Stock Prices: Eastman Kodak Co.; symbol: EK; exchange: New York Stock Exchange; end of month closing price; adjusted for stock splits; from December 1986.
Source: Commodity Systems, Inc.
Code: STOCK016P

AH Common Stock Dividends: Eastman Kodak Co.; symbol: EK; exchange: New York Stock Exchange; from December 1986.
Source: Commodity Systems, Inc.
Code: STOCK016D

AI Common Stock Prices: FPL Group, Inc., HLDG; symbol: FPL; exchange: New York Stock Exchange; end of month closing price; adjusted for stock splits; from December 1986.
Source: Commodity Systems, Inc.
Code: STOCK017P

AJ Common Stock Dividends: FPL Group, Inc., HLDG; symbol: FPL; exchange: New York Stock Exchange; from December 1986.
Source: Commodity Systems, Inc.
Code: STOCK017D

AK   Common Stock Prices: General Electric Co.; symbol: GE; exchange: New York Stock Exchange; end of month closing price; adjusted for stock splits; from December 1986.
Source: Commodity Systems, Inc.
Code: STOCK018P

AL   Common Stock Dividends: General Electric Co.; symbol: GE; exchange: New York Stock Exchange; from December 1986.
Source: Commodity Systems, Inc.
Code: STOCK018D

AM   Common Stock Prices: General Motors Cp.; symbol: GM; exchange: New York Stock Exchange; end of month closing price; adjusted for stock splits; from December 1986.
Source: Commodity Systems, Inc.
Code: STOCK019P

AN   Common Stock Dividends: General Motors Cp.; symbol: GM; exchange: New York Stock Exchange; from December 1986.
Source: Commodity Systems, Inc.
Code: STOCK019D

AO   Common Stock Prices: Genentech; symbol: GNE; exchange: New York Stock Exchange; end of month closing price; adjusted for stock splits; from December 1986.
Source: Commodity Systems, Inc.
Code: STOCK020P

AP   Common Stock Dividends: Genentech; symbol: GNE; exchange: New York Stock Exchange; from December 1986.
Source: Commodity Systems, Inc.
Code: STOCK020D

AQ   Common Stock Prices: Goodyear Tire & Rubber; symbol: GT; exchange: New York Stock Exchange; end of month closing price; adjusted for stock splits; from December 1986.
Source: Commodity Systems, Inc.
Code: STOCK021P

AR   Common Stock Dividends: Goodyear Tire & Rubber; symbol: GT; exchange: New York Stock Exchange; from December 1986.
Source: Commodity Systems, Inc.
Code: STOCK021D

AS Common Stock Prices: Home Depot; symbol: HD; exchange: New York Stock Exchange; end of month closing price; adjusted for stock splits; from December 1986.
Source: Commodity Systems, Inc.
Code: STOCK022P

AT Common Stock Dividends: Home Depot; symbol: HD; exchange: New York Stock Exchange; from December 1986.
Source: Commodity Systems, Inc.
Code: STOCK022D

AU Common Stock Prices: Homestake Mining Co.; symbol: HM; exchange: New York Stock Exchange; end of month closing price; adjusted for stock splits; from December 1986.
Source: Commodity Systems, Inc.
Code: STOCK023P

AV Common Stock Dividends: Homestake Mining Co.; symbol: HM; exchange: New York Stock Exchange; from December 1986.
Source: Commodity Systems, Inc.
Code: STOCK023D

AW Common Stock Prices: Hewlett-Packard Co.; symbol: HWP; exchange: New York Stock Exchange; end of month closing price; adjusted for stock splits; from December 1986.
Source: Commodity Systems, Inc.
Code: STOCK024P

AX Common Stock Dividends: Hewlett-Packard Co.; symbol: HWP; exchange: New York Stock Exchange; from December 1986.
Source: Commodity Systems, Inc.
Code: STOCK024D

AY Common Stock Prices: Intl Business Machines; symbol: IBM; exchange: New York Stock Exchange; end of month closing price; adjusted for stock splits; from December 1986.
Source: Commodity Systems, Inc.
Code: STOCK025P

AZ Common Stock Dividends: Intl Business Machines; symbol: IBM; exchange: New York Stock Exchange; from December 1986.
Source: Commodity Systems, Inc.
Code: STOCK025D

BA   Common Stock Prices: Intl Paper Company; symbol: IP; exchange: New York Stock Exchange; end of month closing price; adjusted for stock splits; from December 1986.
Source: Commodity Systems, Inc.
Code: STOCK026P

BB   Common Stock Dividends: Intl Paper Company; symbol: IP; exchange: New York Stock Exchange; from December 1986.
Source: Commodity Systems, Inc.
Code: STOCK026D

BC   Common Stock Prices: Morgan (JP) & Co.; symbol: JPM; exchange: New York Stock Exchange; end of month closing price; adjusted for stock splits; from December 1986.
Source: Commodity Systems, Inc.
Code: STOCK027P

BD   Common Stock Dividends: Morgan (JP) & Co.; symbol: JPM; exchange: New York Stock Exchange; from December 1986.
Source: Commodity Systems, Inc.
Code: STOCK027D

BE   Common Stock Prices: Kellogg Co.; symbol: K; exchange: New York Stock Exchange; end of month closing price; adjusted for stock splits; from December 1986.
Source: Commodity Systems, Inc.
Code: STOCK028P

BF   Common Stock Dividends: Kellogg Co.; symbol: K; exchange: New York Stock Exchange; from December 1986.
Source: Commodity Systems, Inc.
Code: STOCK028D

BG   Common Stock Prices: Coca Cola Co.; symbol: KO; exchange: New York Stock Exchange; end of month closing price; adjusted for stock splits; from December 1986.
Source: Commodity Systems, Inc.
Code: STOCK029P

BH   Common Stock Dividends: Coca Cola Co.; symbol: KO; exchange: New York Stock Exchange; from December 1986.
Source: Commodity Systems, Inc.
Code: STOCK029D

BI Common Stock Prices: McDonald's Corp.; symbol: MCD; exchange: New York Stock Exchange; end of month closing price; adjusted for stock splits; from December 1986.
Source: Commodity Systems, Inc.
Code: STOCK030P

BJ Common Stock Dividends: McDonald's Corp.; symbol: MCD; exchange: New York Stock Exchange; from December 1986.
Source: Commodity Systems, Inc.
Code: STOCK030D

BK Common Stock Prices: MCI Communications; symbol: MCIC; exchange: NASDAQ; end of month closing price; adjusted for stock splits; from December 1986.
Source: Commodity Systems, Inc.
Code: STOCK031P

BL Common Stock Dividends: MCI Communications; symbol: MCIC; exchange: NASDAQ; from December 1986.
Source: Commodity Systems, Inc.
Code: STOCK031D

BM Common Stock Prices: Minnesota Mining/Mfg.; symbol: MMM; exchange: New York Stock Exchange; end of month closing price; adjusted for stock splits; from December 1986.
Source: Commodity Systems, Inc.
Code: STOCK032P

BN Common Stock Dividends: Minnesota Mining/Mfg.; symbol: MMM; exchange: New York Stock Exchange; from December 1986.
Source: Commodity Systems, Inc.
Code: STOCK032D

BO Common Stock Prices: Philip Morris, Inc.; symbol: MO; exchange: New York Stock Exchange; end of month closing price; adjusted for stock splits; from December 1986.
Source: Commodity Systems, Inc.
Code: STOCK033P

BP Common Stock Dividends: Philip Morris, Inc.; symbol: MO; exchange: New York Stock Exchange; from December 1986.
Source: Commodity Systems, Inc.
Code: STOCK033D

BQ   Common Stock Prices: Merck & Co. Inc.; symbol: MRK; exchange: New York Stock Exchange; end of month closing price; adjusted for stock splits; from December 1986.
Source: Commodity Systems, Inc.
Code: STOCK034P

BR   Common Stock Dividends: Merck & Co. Inc.; symbol: MRK; exchange: New York Stock Exchange; from December 1986.
Source: Commodity Systems, Inc.
Code: STOCK034D

BS   Common Stock Prices: Microsoft Cp.; symbol: MSFT; exchange: NASDAQ; end of month closing price; adjusted for stock splits; from December 1986.
Source: Commodity Systems, Inc.
Code: STOCK035P

BT   Common Stock Dividends: Microsoft Cp.; symbol: MSFT; exchange: NASDAQ; from December 1986.
Source: Commodity Systems, Inc.
Code: STOCK035D

BU   Common Stock Prices: Novell, Inc.; symbol: NOVL; exchange: NASDAQ; end of month closing price; adjusted for stock splits; from August 1988.
Source: Commodity Systems, Inc.
Code: STOCK036P

BV   Common Stock Dividends: Novell, Inc.; symbol: NOVL; exchange: NASDAQ; from August 1988.
Source: Commodity Systems, Inc.
Code: STOCK036D

BW   Common Stock Prices: Pepsi Co., Inc.; symbol: PEP; exchange: New York Stock Exchange; end of month closing price; adjusted for stock splits; from December 1986.
Source: Commodity Systems, Inc.
Code: STOCK037P

BX   Common Stock Dividends: Pepsi Co., Inc.; symbol: PEP; exchange: New York Stock Exchange; from December 1986.
Source: Commodity Systems, Inc.
Code: STOCK037D

BY Common Stock Prices: Procter & Gamble Co.; symbol: PG; exchange: New York Stock Exchange; end of month closing price; adjusted for stock splits; from December 1986.
Source: Commodity Systems, Inc.
Code: STOCK038P

BZ Common Stock Dividends: Procter & Gamble Co.; Inc.; symbol: PG; exchange: New York Stock Exchange; from December 1986.
Source: Commodity Systems, Inc.
Code: STOCK038D

CA Common Stock Prices: PaineWebber Group; symbol: PWJ; exchange: New York Stock Exchange; end of month closing price; adjusted for stock splits; from December 1986.
Source: Commodity Systems, Inc.
Code: STOCK039P

CB Common Stock Dividends: PaineWebber Group; symbol: PWJ; exchange: New York Stock Exchange; from December 1986.
Source: Commodity Systems, Inc.
Code: STOCK039D

CC Common Stock Prices: Pennzoil Co.; symbol: PZL; exchange: New York Stock Exchange; end of month closing price; adjusted for stock splits; from December 1986.
Source: Commodity Systems, Inc.
Code: STOCK040P

CD Common Stock Dividends: Pennzoil; symbol: PZL; exchange: New York Stock Exchange; from December 1986.
Source: Commodity Systems, Inc.
Code: STOCK040D

CE Common Stock Prices: Ryder System; symbol: R; exchange: New York Stock Exchange; end of month closing price; adjusted for stock splits; from December 1986.
Source: Commodity Systems, Inc.
Code: STOCK041P

CF Common Stock Dividends: Ryder System; symbol: R; exchange: New York Stock Exchange; from December 1986.
Source: Commodity Systems, Inc.
Code: STOCK041D

CG   Common Stock Prices: Sears Roebuck & Co.; symbol: S; exchange: New York Stock Exchange; end of month closing price; adjusted for stock splits; from December 1986.
Source: Commodity Systems, Inc.
Code: STOCK042P

CH   Common Stock Dividends: Sears Roebuck & Co.; symbol: S; exchange: New York Stock Exchange; from December 1986.
Source: Commodity Systems, Inc.
Code: STOCK042D

CI   Common Stock Prices: Charles Schwab; symbol: SCH; exchange: New York Stock Exchange; end of month closing price; adjusted for stock splits; from June 1989.
Source: Commodity Systems, Inc.
Code: STOCK043P

CJ   Common Stock Dividends: Charles Schwab; symbol: SCH; exchange: New York Stock Exchange; from June 1989.
Source: Commodity Systems, Inc.
Code: STOCK043D

CK   Common Stock Prices: Sunshine Mining Co.; symbol: SSC; exchange: New York Stock Exchange; end of month closing price; adjusted for stock splits; from December 1986.
Source: Commodity Systems, Inc.
Code: STOCK044P

CL   Common Stock Dividends: Sunshine Mining Co.; symbol: SSC; exchange: New York Stock Exchange; from December 1986.
Source: Commodity Systems, Inc.
Code: STOCK044D

CM   Common Stock Prices: American Telephone & Telegraph; symbol: T; exchange: New York Stock Exchange; end of month closing price; adjusted for stock splits; from December 1986.
Source: Commodity Systems, Inc.
Code: STOCK045P

CN   Common Stock Dividends: American Telephone & Telegraph; symbol: T; exchange: New York Stock Exchange; from December 1986.
Source: Commodity Systems, Inc.
Code: STOCK045D

CO   Common Stock Prices: Texaco, Inc.; symbol: TX; exchange: New York Stock Exchange; end of month closing price; adjusted for stock splits; from December 1986.
Source: Commodity Systems, Inc.
Code: STOCK046P

CP   Common Stock Dividends: Texaco, Inc.; symbol: TX; exchange: New York Stock Exchange; from December 1986.
Source: Commodity Systems, Inc.
Code: STOCK046D

CQ   Common Stock Prices: UAL, Inc.; symbol: UAL; exchange: New York Stock Exchange; end of month closing price; adjusted for stock splits; from December 1986.
Source: Commodity Systems, Inc.
Code: STOCK047P

CR   Common Stock Dividends: UAL, Inc.; symbol: UAL; exchange: New York Stock Exchange; from December 1986.
Source: Commodity Systems, Inc.
Code: STOCK047D

CS   Common Stock Prices: Union Carbide Cp; symbol: UK; exchange: New York Stock Exchange; end of month closing price; adjusted for stock splits; from December 1986.
Source: Commodity Systems, Inc.
Code: STOCK048P

CT   Common Stock Dividends: Union Carbide Cp; symbol: UK; exchange: New York Stock Exchange; from December 1986.
Source: Commodity Systems, Inc.
Code: STOCK048D

CU   Common Stock Prices: The Upjohn Co.; symbol: UPJ; exchange: New York Stock Exchange; end of month closing price; adjusted for stock splits; from December 1986.
Source: Commodity Systems, Inc.
Code: STOCK049P

CV   Common Stock Dividends: The Upjohn Co.; symbol: UPJ; exchange: New York Stock Exchange; from December 1986.
Source: Commodity Systems, Inc.
Code: STOCK049D

CW   Common Stock Prices: United Technologies; symbol: UTX; exchange: New York Stock Exchange; end of month closing price; adjusted for stock splits; from December 1986.
Source: Commodity Systems, Inc.
Code: STOCK050P

CX   Common Stock Dividends: United Technologies; symbol: UTX; exchange: New York Stock Exchange; from December 1986.
Source: Commodity Systems, Inc.
Code: STOCK050D

CY   Common Stock Prices: Winn-Dixie Stores; Inc., symbol: WIN; exchange: New York Stock Exchange; end of month closing price; adjusted for stock splits; from December 1986.
Source: Commodity Systems, Inc.
Code: STOCK051P

CZ   Common Stock Dividends: Winn-Dixie Stores, Inc.; symbol: WIN; exchange: New York Stock Exchange; from December 1986.
Source: Commodity Systems, Inc.
Code: STOCK051D

DA   Common Stock Prices: Wal-Mart; symbol: WMT; exchange: New York Stock Exchange; end of month closing price; adjusted for stock splits; from December 1986.
Source: Commodity Systems, Inc.
Code: STOCK052P

DB   Common Stock Dividends: Wal-Mart; symbol: WMT; exchange: New York Stock Exchange; from December 1986.
Source: Commodity Systems, Inc.
Code: STOCK052D

DC   Common Stock Prices: Waste Management, Inc.; symbol: WMX; exchange: New York Stock Exchange; end of month closing price; adjusted for stock splits; from December 1986.
Source: Commodity Systems, Inc.
Code: STOCK053P

DD   Common Stock Dividends: Waste Management, Inc.; symbol: WMX; exchange: New York Stock Exchange; from December 1986.
Source: Commodity Systems, Inc.
Code: STOCK053D

DE   Common Stock Prices: Westinghouse Electric; symbol: WX; exchange: New York Stock Exchange; end of month closing price; adjusted for stock splits; from December 1986.
Source: Commodity Systems, Inc.
Code: STOCK054P

DF   Common Stock Dividends: Westinghouse Electric; symbol: WX; exchange: New York Stock Exchange; from December 1986.
Source: Commodity Systems, Inc.
Code: STOCK054D

DG   Common Stock Prices: Exxon Cp; symbol: XON; exchange: New York Stock Exchange; end of month closing price; adjusted for stock splits; from December 1986.
Source: Commodity Systems, Inc.
Code: STOCK055P

DH   Common Stock Dividends: Exxon Cp; symbol: XON; exchange: New York Stock Exchange; from December 1986.
Source: Commodity Systems, Inc.
Code: STOCK055D

DI   Common Stock Prices: Xerox Cp; symbol: XRX; exchange: New York Stock Exchange; end of month closing price; adjusted for stock splits; from December 1986.
Source: Commodity Systems, Inc.
Code: STOCK056P

DJ   Common Stock Dividends: Xerox Cp; symbol: XRX; exchange: New York Stock Exchange; from December 1986.
Source: Commodity Systems, Inc.
Code: STOCK056D

DK   Common Stock Prices: Woolworth Co.; symbol: Z; exchange: New York Stock Exchange; end of month closing price; adjusted for stock splits; from December 1986.
Source: Commodity Systems, Inc.
Code: STOCK057P

DL   Common Stock Dividends: Woolworth Co.; symbol: Z; exchange: New York Stock Exchange; from December 1986.
Source: Commodity Systems, Inc.
Code: STOCK057D

Money Market Yields
Spreadsheet: MONEYYLD.WK1   Monthly Data

A   Year of the observation
Code: MMYYR

B   Month of the observation (1 = January; 2 = February; etc.)
Code: MMYMO

C   Federal Funds (weighted average of rates on trades, average of daily figures, percent per annum); from January 1970.
Source: *Federal Reserve Bulletin*, Table 1.35, various issues.
Code: MMY001

D   Discount window borrowing (average of daily figures, rate for the Federal Reserve Bank of New York); from January 1970.
Source: *Federal Reserve Bulletin*, Table 1.35, various issues.
Code: MMY002

E   Commercial paper: 1-month (annualized, quoted on a discount basis, an average of rates for firms whose bond rating is AA or the equivalent); from April 1971.
Source: *Federal Reserve Bulletin*, Table 1.35, various issues.
Code: MMY003

F   Commercial paper: 3-month (annualized, quoted on a discount basis, an average of rates for firms whose bond rating is AA or the equivalent); from April 1971.
Source: *Federal Reserve Bulletin*, Table 1.35, various issues.
Code: MMY004

G   Commercial paper: 6-month (annualized, quoted on a discount basis, an average of rates for firms whose bond rating is AA or the equivalent); from January 1970.
Source: *Federal Reserve Bulletin*, Table 1.35, various issues.
Code: MMY005

H   Commercial Paper Outstanding, Total, Financial and Non-Financial Companies; thousands of dollars; seasonally adjusted; from January 1983.
Source: Federal Reserve Bank of New York, Domestic Reports Division, News Release—Commercial Paper in the United States, various issues.
Code: MMY006

I   Commercial Paper Outstanding, Financial Companies; thousands of dollars; seasonally adjusted; from January 1983.
    Source: Federal Reserve Bank of New York, Domestic Reports Division, News Release—Commercial Paper in the United States, various issues.
    Code: MMY007

J   Commercial Paper Outstanding, Nonfinancial Companies; millions of dollars; seasonally adjusted; from January 1970.
    Source: Federal Reserve Bank of New York, Domestic Reports Division, News Release—Commercial Paper in the United States, various issues.
    Code: MMY008

K   Bankers' Acceptances: 3-month (annualized, quoted on a discount basis, representative closing yields for acceptances of the highest rated money center banks); from January 1970.
    Source: *Federal Reserve Bulletin*, Table 1.35, various issues.
    Code: MMY009

L   Bankers' Acceptances: 6-month (annualized, quoted on a discount basis, representative closing yields for acceptances of the highest rated money center banks); from January 1981.
    Source: *Federal Reserve Bulletin*, Table 1.35, various issues.
    Code: MMY010

M   Certificates of Deposit, secondary market: 1-month (annualized, an average of dealer offering rates on nationally traded certificates of deposit); from January 1970.
    Source: *Federal Reserve Bulletin*, Table 1.35, various issues.
    Code: MMY011

N   Certificates of Deposit, secondary market: 3-month (annualized, an average of dealer offering rates on nationally traded certificates of deposit); from January 1970.
    Source: *Federal Reserve Bulletin*, Table 1.35, various issues.
    Code: MMY012

O   Certificates of Deposit, secondary market: 6-month (annualized, an average of dealer offering rates on nationally traded certificates of deposit); from January 1970.
    Source: *Federal Reserve Bulletin*, Table 1.35, various issues.
    Code: MMY013

P   Eurodollar Deposit Rate (London); 7-Day; average of weekly averages week ending Wednesday; percent per annum; from January 1971.
          Source: Board of Governors of the Federal Reserve System, Division of International Finance, Selected Interest and Exchange Rates—Weekly Series of Charts—Chart 6, various issues.
          Code: MMY014

Q   Eurodollar Deposit Rate (London); 1-Month; average of weekly averages week ending Wednesday; percent per annum; from January 1970.
          Source: Board of Governors of the Federal Reserve System, Division of International Finance, Selected Interest and Exchange Rates—Weekly Series of Charts—Chart 6, various issues.
          Code: MMY015

R   Eurodollar Deposit Rate (London); 3-Month; average of weekly averages week ending Wednesday; percent per annum; from January 1970.
          Source: Board of Governors of the Federal Reserve System, Division of International Finance, Selected Interest and Exchange Rates—Weekly Series of Charts—Chart 6, various issues.
          Code: MMY016

S   Eurodollar Deposit Rate (London); 6-Month; average of weekly averages week ending Wednesday; percent per annum; from January 1970.
          Source: Board of Governors of the Federal Reserve System, Division of International Finance, Selected Interest and Exchange Rates—Weekly Series of Charts—Chart 6, various issues.
          Code: MMY017

T   Eurodollar Deposit Rate (London); 1 Year; average of weekly averages week ending Wednesday; percent per annum; from January 1971.
          Source: Board of Governors of the Federal Reserve System, Division of International Finance, Selected Interest and Exchange Rates—Weekly Series of Charts—Chart 6, various issues.
          Code: MMY018

U   U.S. Treasury bills; secondary market; 3-month; percent per annum; monthly average of daily figures; from January 1970.
          Source: *Federal Reserve Bulletin*, Table 1.35, various issues.
          Code: MMY019

V   U.S. Treasury bills; secondary market; 6-month; percent per annum; monthly average of daily figures; from January 1970.
          Source: *Federal Reserve Bulletin*, Table 1.35, various issues.
          Code: MMY020

W   U.S. Treasury bills; secondary market; 1 Year; percent per annum; monthly
     average of daily figures; from January 1970.
     Source: *Federal Reserve Bulletin*, Table 1.35, various issues.
     Code: MMY021

X   U.S. Treasury bills; Auction Average; Discount (Issue Date); 3-Month Bill;
     average of daily figures; from January 1970.
     Source: *Federal Reserve Bulletin*, Table 1.35, various issues.
     Code: MMY022

Y   U.S. Treasury bills; Auction Average; Discount (Issue Date); 6-Month Bill;
     average of daily figures; from January 1970.
     Source: *Federal Reserve Bulletin*, Table 1.35, various issues.
     Code: MMY023

Z   U.S. Treasury bills; Auction Average; Discount (Issue Date); 1-Year Bill;
     average of daily figures; from January 1970.
     Source: *Federal Reserve Bulletin*, Table 1.35, various issues.
     Code: MMY024

Foreign Money Market Rates
Spreadsheet: FORMONEY.WK1   Monthly Data

A   Year of the observation
     Code: FMMRYR

B   Month of the observation (1 = January; 2 = February; etc.)
     Code: FMMRMO

C   Foreign Short-Term Interest Rates; Official Discount Rate; Austria; average of
     daily figures; percent per year; from January 1970.
     Source: Organization for Economic Cooperation and Development.
     Code: FMMR001

D   Foreign Short-Term Interest Rates; Official Discount Rate; Belgium; average
     of daily figures; percent per year; from January 1970.
     Source: Organization for Economic Cooperation and Development.
     Code: FMMR002

E   Foreign Short-Term Interest Rates; 90 day Deposit Receipts; Canada; average
     of daily figures; percent per year; from January 1970.
     Source: Organization for Economic Cooperation and Development.
     Code: FMMR003

F   Foreign Short-Term Interest Rates; Official Discount Rate; Denmark; average of daily figures; percent per year; from January 1970.
Source: Organization for Economic Cooperation and Development.
Code: FMMR004

G   Foreign Short-Term Interest Rates; Official Discount Rate; Finland; average of daily figures; percent per year; from January 1970.
Source: Organization for Economic Cooperation and Development.
Code: FMMR005

H   Foreign Short-Term Interest Rates; Official Discount Rate; France; average of daily figures; percent per year; from January 1970.
Source: Organization for Economic Cooperation and Development.
Code: FMMR006

I   Foreign Short-Term Interest Rates; Official Discount Rate; Germany; average of daily figures; percent per year; from January 1970.
Source: Organization for Economic Cooperation and Development.
Code: FMMR007

J   Foreign Short-Term Interest Rates; Prime Bank Bills (3 months); Great Britain; average of daily figures; percent per year; from January 1970.
Source: Organization for Economic Cooperation and Development.
Code: FMMR008

K   Foreign Short-Term Interest Rates; Official Discount Rate; Ireland; average of daily figures; percent per year; from January 1970.
Source: Organization for Economic Cooperation and Development.
Code: FMMR009

L   Foreign Short-Term Interest Rates; Official Discount Rate; Italy; average of daily figures; percent per year; from January 1970.
Source: Organization for Economic Cooperation and Development.
Code: FMMR010

M   Foreign Short-Term Interest Rates; Official Discount Rate; Japan; average of daily figures; percent per year; from January 1970.
Source: Organization for Economic Cooperation and Development.
Code: FMMR011

N   Foreign Short-Term Interest Rates; Official Discount Rate; Netherlands; average of daily figures; percent per year; from January 1970.
Source: Organization for Economic Cooperation and Development.
Code: FMMR012

O   Foreign Short-Term Interest Rates; Official Discount Rate; Spain; average of daily figures; percent per year; from January 1970.
Source: Organization for Economic Cooperation and Development.
Code: FMMR013

P   Foreign Short-Term Interest Rates; Official Discount Rate; Sweden; average of daily figures; percent per year; from January 1970.
Source: Organization for Economic Cooperation and Development.
Code: FMMR014

Q   Foreign Short-Term Interest Rates; Official Discount Rate; Switzerland; average of daily figures; percent per year; from January 1970.
Source: Organization for Economic Cooperation and Development.
Code: FMMR015

R   Foreign Short-Term Interest Rates; Official Discount Rate; United States; average of daily figures; percent per year; from January 1970.
Source: Organization for Economic Cooperation and Development.
Code: FMMR016

S   Foreign Short-Term Interest Rates; Prime Rate; United States; average of daily figures; percent per year; from January 1970.
Source: Organization for Economic Cooperation and Development.
Code: FMMR017

Bond Market Prices, Yields, and Activity
Spreadsheet: BONDYLD.WK1 Monthly Data

A   Year of the observation
     Code: BYLDYR

B   Month of the observation (1 = January; 2 = February; etc.)
     Code: BYLDMO

C   U.S. Treasury Notes and Bonds; constant maturities; 2-year (yields on actively traded issues adjusted to constant maturities); monthly average of daily figures; from June 1976.
     Source: *Federal Reserve Bulletin*, Table 1.35, various issues.
     Code: BYLD001

D   U.S. Treasury Notes and Bonds; constant maturities; 3-year (yields on actively traded issues adjusted to constant maturities); from January 1970.
     Source: *Federal Reserve Bulletin*, Table 1.35, various issues.
     Code: BYLD002

E   U.S. Treasury Notes and Bonds; constant maturities; 5-year (yields on actively traded issues adjusted to constant maturities); from January 1970.
     Source: *Federal Reserve Bulletin*, Table 1.35, various issues.
     Code: BYLD003

F   U.S. Treasury Notes and Bonds; constant maturities; 7-year (yields on actively traded issues adjusted to constant maturities); from January 1970.
     Source: *Federal Reserve Bulletin*, Table 1.35, various issues.
     Code: BYLD004

G   U.S. Treasury Notes and Bonds; constant maturities; 10-year (yields on actively traded issues adjusted to constant maturities); from January 1970.
     Source: *Federal Reserve Bulletin*, Table 1.35, various issues.
     Code: BYLD005

H   U.S. Treasury Notes and Bonds; constant maturities; 30-year (yields on actively traded issues adjusted to constant maturities); from March 1977.
     Source: *Federal Reserve Bulletin*, Table 1.35, various issues.
     Code: BYLD006

I   U.S. Treasury Notes and Bonds; composite; over 10 years (long-term); (unweighted average of rates on all outstanding bonds neither due nor callable in less than 10 years, including flower bonds); from January 1970.
     Source: *Federal Reserve Bulletin*, Table 1.35, various issues.
     Code: BYLD007

J   U.S. Treasury Notes and Bonds; Market Yield on Long-Term Treasury Bonds (10+ years); percent per annum; from January 1970.
     Source: U.S. Department of the Treasury, *Treasury Bulletin*, Table 1.35, various issues.
     Code: BYLD008

K   Composite Municipal Bond Yield (20 Year); percent per annum; average of daily figures; from January 1986.
     Source: Moody's Investors Service, *Bond Survey*, various issues.
     Code: BYLD009

L   AAA Municipal Bond Yield (20 Year); percent per annum; average of daily figures; from January 1970.
     Source: Moody's Investors Service, *Bond Survey*, various issues.
     Code: BYLD010

M   AAA Municipal Bond Yield (10 Year); percent per annum; average of daily figures; from January 1986.
     Source: Moody's Investors Service, *Bond Survey*, various issues.
     Code: BYLD011

N   AA Municipal Bond Yield (20 Year); percent per annum; average of daily figures; from January 1986.
     Source: Moody's Investors Service, *Bond Survey*, various issues.
     Code: BYLD012

O   AA Municipal Bond Yield (10 Year); percent per annum; average of daily figures; from January 1986.
     Source: Moody's Investors Service, *Bond Survey*, various issues.
     Code: BYLD013

P   A Municipal Bond Yield (20 Year); percent per annum; average of daily figures; from January 1986.
     Source: Moody's Investors Service, *Bond Survey*, various issues.
     Code: BYLD014

Q   BAA Municipal Bond Yield (20 Year); percent per annum; average of daily figures; from January 1986.
     Source: Moody's Investors Service, *Bond Survey*, various issues.
     Code: BYLD015

R   AAA Corporate Bonds, Average Yield; average of daily figures; percent per annum; from January 1970.
     Source: Moody's Investors Service, *Bond Survey*, various issues.
     Code: BYLD016

S   AA Corporate Bonds, Average Yield; average of daily figures; percent per annum; from January 1970.
Source: Moody's Investors Service, *Bond Survey*, various issues.
Code: BYLD017

T   A Corporate Bonds, Average Yield; average of daily figures; percent per annum; from January 1970.
Source: Moody's Investors Service, *Bond Survey*, various issues.
Code: BYLD018

U   BAA Corporate Bonds, Average Yield; average of daily figures; percent per annum; from January 1970.
Source: Moody's Investors Service, *Bond Survey*, various issues.
Code: BYLD019

V   Average Yield on Corporate Bonds; average of daily figures; percent per annum; from January 1970.
Source: Moody's Investors Service, *Bond Survey*, various issues.
Code: BYLD020

W   AAA Industrial Bonds, Average Yield; average of daily figures; percent per annum; from January 1970.
Source: Moody's Investors Service, *Bond Survey*, various issues.
Code: BYLD021

X   AA Industrial Bonds, Average Yield; average of daily figures; percent per annum; from January 1970.
Source: Moody's Investors Service, *Bond Survey*, various issues.
Code: BYLD022

Y   A Industrial Bonds, Average Yield; average of daily figures; percent per annum; from January 1970.
Source: Moody's Investors Service, *Bond Survey*, various issues.
Code: BYLD023

Z   BAA Industrial Bonds, Average Yield; average of daily figures; percent per annum; from January 1970.
Source: Moody's Investors Service, *Bond Survey*, various issues.
Code: BYLD024

AA   Average Yield on Industrial Bonds; average of daily figures; percent per annum; from January 1970.
Source: Moody's Investors Service, *Bond Survey*, various issues.
Code: BYLD025

AB AA Utility Bonds, Average Yield; average of daily figures; percent per annum; from January 1970.
Source: Moody's Investors Service, *Bond Survey*, various issues.
Code: BYLD026

AC A Utility Bonds, Average Yield; average of daily figures; percent per annum; from January 1970.
Source: Moody's Investors Service, *Bond Survey*, various issues.
Code: BYLD027

AD BAA Utility Bonds, Average Yield; average of daily figures; percent per annum; from January 1970.
Source: Moody's Investors Service, *Bond Survey*, various issues.
Code: BYLD028

AE Average Yield on Public Utility Bonds; average of daily figures; percent per annum; from January 1970.
Source: Moody's Investors Service, *Bond Survey*, various issues.
Code: BYLD029

Foreign Bond Yields and Performance
Spreadsheet: FORBOND.WK1   Monthly Data

A   Year of the observation
Code: FBONDYR

B   Month of the observation (1 = January; 2 = February; etc.)
Code: FBONDMO

C   Interest Rates on Foreign Government Treasury Securities; 15-year Commonwealth Government Bonds; Australia; percent per year; from January 1982.
Source: Organization for Economic Cooperation and Development.
Code: FBOND001

D   Interest Rates on Foreign Government Treasury Securities, Public Sector Bonds (greater than 1 year); Austria; percent per year; from January 1970.
Source: Organization for Economic Cooperation and Development.
Code: FBOND002

E   Interest Rates on Foreign Government Treasury Securities, Central Government Bonds (greater than 5 years); Belgium; percent per year; from January 1970.
Source: Organization for Economic Cooperation and Development.
Code: FBOND003

F   Interest Rates on Foreign Government Treasury Securities, Federal Government Bonds (greater than 10 years); Canada; percent per year; from January 1970.
Source: Organization for Economic Cooperation and Development.
Code: FBOND004

G   Interest Rates on Foreign Government Treasury Securities, Public and Semi-Public Sector Bonds; last Friday of month; France; percent per year; from January 1970.
Source: Organization for Economic Cooperation and Development.
Code: FBOND005

H   Interest Rates on Foreign Government Treasury Securities; 7-15 year Public Sector Bonds; Germany; percent per year; from January 1973.
Source: Organization for Economic Cooperation and Development.
Code: FBOND006

I   Interest Rates on Foreign Government Treasury Securities, Central Government Bonds; greater than 20 years; Great Britain; percent per year; from January 1970.
Source: Organization for Economic Cooperation and Development.
Code: FBOND007

J   Interest Rates on Foreign Government Treasury Securities, Central Government Bonds; last Friday of month; 5 year; Ireland; percent per year; from January 1971.
Source: Organization for Economic Cooperation and Development
Code: FBOND008

K   Interest Rates on Foreign Government Treasury Securities, Treasury Bonds; 6 year average maturity; Italy; percent per year; from January 1970.
Source: Organization for Economic Cooperation and Development.
Code: FBOND009

L   Interest Rates on Foreign Government Treasury Securities, Central Government Bonds; end of month rates; Japan; percent per year; from January 1970.
Source: Organization for Economic Cooperation and Development.
Code: FBOND010

M   Interest Rates on Foreign Government Treasury Securities, Central Government Bonds (greater than 2 years); Spain; percent per year; from January 1988.
Source: Organization for Economic Cooperation and Development.
Code: FBOND011

N Interest Rates on Foreign Government Treasury Securities, Central Government Bonds; 10 year; Sweden; percent per year; from January 1987.
Source: Organization for Economic Cooperation and Development.
Code: FBOND012

O Interest Rates on Foreign Government Treasury Securities, Confederation Bonds; last Friday of month; 5 year; Switzerland; percent per year; from January 1970.
Source: Organization for Economic Cooperation and Development.
Code: FBOND013

P World Government Bond Performance Indexes: Salomon Brothers World Government Bond Index; total rate of return; remaining maturities of at least one year; stated in local currency terms; from January 1985.
Source: Salomon Brothers, Inc., Global Fixed-Income Research.
Code: FBOND014

Q World Government Bond Performance Indexes: Salomon Brothers Non-U.S. World Government Bond Index; total rate of return; remaining maturities of at least one year; stated in local currency terms; from January 1985.
Source: Salomon Brothers, Inc., Global Fixed-Income Research.
Code: FBOND015

R World Government Bond Performance Indexes: Salomon Brothers U.S. Government Bond Index; total rate of return; remaining maturities of at least one year; stated in local currency terms; from January 1985.
Source: Salomon Brothers, Inc., Global Fixed-Income Research.
Code: FBOND016

S World Government Bond Performance Indexes: Salomon Brothers Canadian Government Bond Index; total rate of return; remaining maturities of at least one year; stated in local currency terms; from January 1985.
Source: Salomon Brothers, Inc., Global Fixed-Income Research.
Code: FBOND017

T World Government Bond Performance Indexes: Salomon Brothers German Government Bond Index; total rate of return; remaining maturities of at least one year; stated in local currency terms; from January 1985.
Source: Salomon Brothers, Inc., Global Fixed-Income Research.
Code: FBOND018

U World Government Bond Performance Indexes: Salomon Brothers Japanese Government Bond Index; total rate of return; remaining maturities of at least one year; stated in local currency terms; from January 1985.
Source: Salomon Brothers, Inc., Global Fixed-Income Research.
Code: FBOND019

V   World Government Bond Performance Indexes: Salomon Brothers United Kingdom Government Bond Index; total rate of return; remaining maturities of at least one year; stated in local currency terms (gilt); from January 1985.
Source: Salomon Brothers, Inc., Global Fixed-Income Research.
Code: FBOND020

W   World Government Bond Performance Indexes: Salomon Brothers Swiss Government Bond Index; total rate of return; remaining maturities of at least one year; stated in local currency terms; from January 1985.
Source: Salomon Brothers, Inc., Global Fixed-Income Research.
Code: FBOND021

X   World Government Bond Performance Indexes: Salomon Brothers Dutch Government Bond Index; total rate of return; remaining maturities of at least one year; stated in local currency terms; from January 1985.
Source: Salomon Brothers, Inc., Global Fixed-Income Research.
Code: FBOND022

Y   World Government Bond Performance Indexes: Salomon Brothers French Government Bond Index; total rate of return; remaining maturities of at least one year; stated in local currency terms; from January 1985.
Source: Salomon Brothers, Inc., Global Fixed-Income Research.
Code: FBOND023

Z   World Government Bond Performance Indexes: Salomon Brothers Australian Government Bond Index; total rate of return; remaining maturities of at least one year; stated in local currency terms; from January 1985.
Source: Salomon Brothers, Inc., Global Fixed-Income Research.
Code: FBOND024

AA   World Government Bond Performance Indexes: Salomon Brothers Danish Government Bond Index; total rate of return; remaining maturities of at least one year; stated in local currency terms; from April 1989.
Source: Salomon Brothers, Inc., Global Fixed-Income Research.
Code: FBOND025

Mortgage Market Prices, Yields, and Activity
Spreadsheet: MORTMKT.WK1   Monthly Data

A   Year of the observation
    Code: MOMKTYR

B   Month of the observation (1 = January; 2 = February; etc.)
    Code: MOMKTMO

C   Secondary Market Yield on FHA Loans; assumed prepayment of mortgages in
    12 years; percent; from January 1970.
    Source: U.S. Department of Housing and Urban Development, Federal
          Housing Administration, *HUD News,* various issues.
    Code: MOMKT001

D   Conventional Home Mortgage Rates; Fixed Rate Loans Closed; percent; from
    July 1982.
    Source: Federal Housing Finance Board, *Federal Housing Finance Board
          News,* various issues.
    Code: MOMKT002

E   Conventional Home Mortgage Rates; Adjustable Rate Loans Closed; percent;
    from July 1982.
    Source: Federal Housing Finance Board, *Federal Housing Finance Board
          News,* various issues.
    Code: MOMKT003

F   Conventional Home Mortgage Rates; Loans Closed; National Average for All
    Major Lenders, percent; from July 1973.
    Source: Federal Housing Finance Board, *Federal Housing Finance Board
          News,* various issues.
    Code: MOMKT004

G   Mortgages by Institution; Federal National Mortgage Association; end of
    month; seasonally adjusted; millions of dollars; from January 1970.
    Source: *Federal Reserve Bulletin,* various tables, various issues.
    Code: MOMKT005

H   Mortgages by Institution; Mutual Savings Banks; end of month; millions of
    dollars; from January 1970.
    Source: *Federal Reserve Bulletin,* various tables, various issues.
    Code: MOMKT006

I   Mortgages by Institution; Life Insurance Companies; end of month; millions of dollars; from January 1970.
Source: *Federal Reserve Bulletin,* various tables, various issues.
Code: MOMKT007

Foreign Exchange
Spreadsheet: FOREX.WK1   Monthly Data

A   Year of the observation
Code: FOEXYR

B   Month of the observation (1 = January; 2 = February; etc.)
Code: FOEXMO

C   Australia (Cents per Australian $); average of daily rates; from January 1970.
Source: Board of Governors of the Federal Reserve System, *Foreign Exchange Rates,* G.5, various issues.
Code: FOEX001

D   Belgium (Belgian Franc per U.S. $); average of daily rates; from January 1970.
Source: Board of Governors of the Federal Reserve System, *Foreign Exchange Rates,* G.5, various issues.
Code: FOEX002

E   Canada (Canadian Dollar per U.S. $); average of daily rates; from January 1970.
Source: Board of Governors of the Federal Reserve System, *Foreign Exchange Rates,* G.5, various issues.
Code: FOEX003

F   Denmark (Danish Krone per U.S. $); average of daily rates; from January 1970.
Source: Board of Governors of the Federal Reserve System, *Foreign Exchange Rates,* G.5, various issues.
Code: FOEX004

G   France (Franc per U.S. $); average of daily rates; from January 1970.
Source: Board of Governors of the Federal Reserve System, *Foreign Exchange Rates,* G.5, various issues.
Code: FOEX005

H   Ireland (Cents per Pound); average of daily rates; from January 1970.
     Source: Board of Governors of the Federal Reserve System, *Foreign Exchange Rates*, G.5, various issues.
     Code: FOEX006

I   Italy (Lira per U.S. $); average of daily rates; from January 1970.
     Source: Board of Governors of the Federal Reserve System, *Foreign Exchange Rates*, G.5, various issues.
     Code: FOEX007

J   Japan (Yen per U.S. $); average of daily rates; from January 1970.
     Source: Board of Governors of the Federal Reserve System, *Foreign Exchange Rates*, G.5, various issues.
     Code: FOEX008

K   Netherlands (Guilder per U.S. $); average of daily rates; from January 1970.
     Source: Board of Governors of the Federal Reserve System, *Foreign Exchange Rates*, G.5, various issues.
     Code: FOEX009

L   Norway (Krone per U.S. $); average of daily rates; from January 1970.
     Source: Board of Governors of the Federal Reserve System, *Foreign Exchange Rates*, G.5, various issues.
     Code: FOEX010

M   South Africa (Cents per Rand); average of daily rates; from January 1970.
     Source: Board of Governors of the Federal Reserve System, *Foreign Exchange Rates*, G.5, various issues.
     Code: FOEX011

N   Sweden (Krona per U.S. $); average of daily rates; from January 1970.
     Source: Board of Governors of the Federal Reserve System, *Foreign Exchange Rates*, G.5, various issues.
     Code: FOEX012

O   Switzerland (Swiss Franc per U.S. $); average of daily rates; from January 1970.
     Source: Board of Governors of the Federal Reserve System, *Foreign Exchange Rates*, G.5, various issues.
     Code: FOEX013

P   United Kingdom (Cents per Pound); average of daily rates; from January 1970.
     Source: Board of Governors of the Federal Reserve System, *Foreign Exchange Rates*, G.5, various issues.
     Code: FOEX014

Q   West Germany (Deutsche Mark per U.S.$); average of daily rates; from January 1970.
     Source: Board of Governors of the Federal Reserve System, *Foreign Exchange Rates,* G.5, various issues.
     Code: FOEX015

R   United States—Index of Weighted Average Exchange Value of U.S. Dollar Against the Currencies of the Industrial Countries; March 1973 = 100; Weights are 1972-76 Average Total Trade Shares of Each of the Industrial Countries; from January 1970.
     Source: Board of Governors of the Federal Reserve System, *Foreign Exchange Rates,* G.5, various issues.
     Code: FOEX016

S   Argentina (Australes per U.S.$); average of daily rates; from January 1976.
     Source: International Monetary Fund, *International Financial Statistics,* various issues.
     Code: FOEX017

T   Brazil (Cruzeiros per U.S.$); average of daily rates; from January 1970.
     Source: International Monetary Fund, *International Financial Statistics,* various issues.
     Code: FOEX018

U   Colombia (Pesos per U.S.$); average of daily rates; from January 1974.
     Source: International Monetary Fund, *International Financial Statistics,* various issues.
     Code: FOEX019

V   Korea (Won per U.S.$); average of daily rates; from January 1970.
     Source: International Monetary Fund, *International Financial Statistics,* various issues.
     Code: FOEX020

W   Mexico (Pesos per U.S.$); average of daily rates; from January 1974.
     Source: International Monetary Fund, *International Financial Statistics,* various issues.
     Code: FOEX021

X   Saudi Arabia (Riyals per U.S.$); average of daily rates; from January 1974.
     Source: International Monetary Fund, *International Financial Statistics,* various issues.
     Code: FOEX022

A Year of the observation
Code: FQUYR

B Quarter of the observation (3 = first quarter; 6 = second quarter; etc.)
Code: FQUQU

C M1: Sum of currency, demand deposits, travelers checks and other checkable deposits; averages of daily figures; billions of dollars; seasonally adjusted; from First Quarter 1959.
Source: Board of Governors of the Federal Reserve System, *Statistical Release: Money Stock Measures and Liquid Assets,* H.6, various issues.
Code: FQU001

D M2: M1 plus overnight RP's and Eurodollars, MMMF balances, MMDA's, and savings and small time deposits; averages of daily figures; billions of dollars; seasonally adjusted; from First Quarter 1959.
Source: Board of Governors of the Federal Reserve System, *Statistical Release: Money Stock Measures and Liquid Assets,* H.6, various issues.
Code: FQU002

E M3: M2 plus large time deposits, term RP's, term Eurodollars, and institution-only MMMF balances; averages of daily figures; billions of dollars; seasonally adjusted; from First Quarter 1959.
Source: Board of Governors of the Federal Reserve System, *Statistical Release: Money Stock Measures and Liquid Assets,* H.6, various issues.
Code: FQU003

F L: M3 plus other liquid assets; averages of daily figures; billions of dollars; seasonally adjusted; from First Quarter 1959.
Source: Board of Governors of the Federal Reserve System, *Statistical Release: Money Stock Measures and Liquid Assets,* H.6, various issues.
Code: FQU004

G Consumer Price Index: All Items (1982-84=100); seasonally adjusted; from First Quarter 1947.
Source: U.S. Department of Labor, Bureau of Labor Statistics, *The Consumer Price Index*, various issues.
Code: FQU005

H   Implicit Price Deflator, Gross National Product, 1987=100; seasonally adjusted; from First Quarter 1947.
Source: *Survey of Current Business,* various issues.
Code: FQU006

I   U.S. Treasury bills; secondary market; 3-month; percent per annum; monthly average of daily figures; from First Quarter 1947.
Source: *Federal Reserve Bulletin,* Table 1.35, various issues.
Code: FQU007

J   U.S. Treasury Notes and Bonds, constant maturities; 30-year (yields on actively traded issues adjusted to constant maturities); from First Quarter 1977.
Source: *Federal Reserve Bulletin,* Table 1.35, various issues.
Code: FQU008

K   AAA Corporate Bonds, Average Yield; average of daily figures; percent per annum; from First Quarter 1947.
Source: Moody's Investors Service, *Bond Survey,* various issues.
Code: FQU009

L   Common Stock Prices: Dow Jones 30 Industrial Stocks; Average of Daily Closing Prices; from First Quarter 1947.
Source: Dow Jones & Company, *The Wall Street Journal,* various issues.
Code: FQU010

M   Common Stock Prices: Standard and Poor's Corporation: Composite (S&P's 500) 1941-43=10; monthly average of daily prices, from First Quarter 1947.
Source: Standard and Poor's Corporation, *The Outlook,* various issues.
Code: FQU011

N   Common Stock Prices: New York Stock Exchange: Composite (1965=50); monthly averages of daily closing rates; from January 1947.
Source: *Federal Reserve Bulletin,* Table 1.36; various issues.
Code: FQU012

3
The
Real
Sector

Macroeconomic Measures

Business Cycle Indicators
Spreadsheet: BUSCYCLE.WK1   Monthly Data

A   Year of the observation
Code: BCYR

B   Month of the observation (1 = January; 2 = February; etc.)
Code: BCMO

C   Composite index: 11 leading indicators; 1982=100; seasonally adjusted; from January 1970.
Source: *Survey of Current Business,* Business Cycle Indicators, various issues.
Code: BC001

D   Components: 11 leading indicators; Avg. Workweek of Production Workers, Mfg.; hours; seasonally adjusted; from January 1970.
Source: *Survey of Current Business,* Business Cycle Indicators, various issues.
Code: BC002

E   Components: 11 leading indicators; Avg. Weekly Initial Claims for Unemployment Insurance State Programs; thousands; seasonally adjusted; from January 1970.
Source: *Survey of Current Business,* Business Cycle Indicators, various issues.
Code: BC003

F   Components: 11 leading indicators; Value of Mgs' New Orders for Consumer Goods & Materials; billions of 1982$; seasonally adjusted; from January 1970.
Source: *Survey of Current Business,* Business Cycle Indicators, various issues.
Code: BC004

G   Components: 11 leading indicators; Index, Stock Prices; 500 Common Stocks, (Standard & Poor's), 1941-43=10; from January 1970.
Source: *Survey of Current Business,* Business Cycle Indicators, various issues.
Code: BC005

H   Components: 11 leading indicators; Contracts and Orders for Plant & Equipment; seasonally adjusted; billions of 1982$; from January 1970.
Source: *Survey of Current Business,* Business Cycle Indicators, various issues.
Code: BC006

I   Components: 11 leading indicators; Index; New Private Housing Units Authorized by Local Building Permit, 1967=100; seasonally adjusted; billions of 1982$; from January 1970.
Source: *Survey of Current Business,* Business Cycle Indicators, various issues.
Code: BC007

J   Components: 11 leading indicators; Vendor Performance; % Companies Reporting Slower Deliveries; from January 1970.
Source: *Survey of Current Business,* Business Cycle Indicators, various issues.
Code: BC008

K   Components: 11 leading indicators; University of Michigan's Index of Consumer Expectations; seasonally adjusted; from January 1970.
Source: *Survey of Current Business,* Business Cycle Indicators, various issues.
Code: BC009

L   Components: 11 leading indicators; Change in Mfg. Unfilled Orders, Durable Goods, Smoothed (weighted 4-term moving average); billions of 1982$; seasonally adjusted; from January 1970.
Source: *Survey of Current Business,* Business Cycle Indicators, various issues.
Code: BC010

M   Components: 11 leading indicators; Change in Sensitive Materials Price (%); Smoothed (weighted 4-term moving average); billions of 1982$; seasonally adjusted; from January 1970.
Source: *Survey of Current Business,* Business Cycle Indicators, various issues.
Code: BC011

N   Components: 11 leading indicators; M-2; Money Supply; billions of 1982$; seasonally adjusted; from January 1970.
Source: *Survey of Current Business,* Business Cycle Indicators, various issues.
Code: BC012

O   Components: 11 leading indicators; Change in Credit - Business and Consumer Borrowing; %; seasonally adjusted; from January 1970.
Source: *Survey of Current Business,* Business Cycle Indicators, various issues.
Code: BC013

P   Components: Capital Investment Commitments; Index of Net Business Formation (1967=100); seasonally adjusted; from January 1970.
Source: *Survey of Current Business,* Business Cycle Indicators, various issues.
Code: BC014

Q   Components: Capital Investment Commitments, Contracts & Orders for Plant & Equipment; billions of 1982$; seasonally adjusted; from January 1970.
Source: *Survey of Current Business,* Business Cycle Indicators, various issues.
Code: BC015

R   Composite Index: 4 Coincident Indicators (1982=100); seasonally adjusted; from January 1970.
Source: *Survey of Current Business,* Business Cycle Indicators, various issues.
Code: BC016

S   Components: 4 Coincident Indicators; Number of Employees on Nonagricultural Payrolls; Establishment Survey; thousands; seasonally adjusted; from January 1970.
Source: *Survey of Current Business,* Business Cycle Indicators, various issues.
Code: BC017

T   Components: 4 Coincident Indicators; Index of Industrial Production; Total (1987=100); seasonally adjusted; from January 1970.
Source: *Survey of Current Business,* Business Cycle Indicators, various issues.
Code: BC018

U   Components: 4 Coincident Indicators; Personal Income Less Transfer Payments; billions of 1987$; seasonally adjusted; from January 1970.
Source: *Survey of Current Business,* Business Cycle Indicators, various issues.
Code: BC019

V   Components: 4 Coincident Indicators, Manufacturing & Trade Sales; millions of 1982$; seasonally adjusted; from January 1970.
Source: *Survey of Current Business,* Business Cycle Indicators, various issues.
Code: BC020

W   Composite Index; 7 Lagging Indicators (1982=100); seasonally adjusted; from January 1970.
Source: *Survey of Current Business,* Business Cycle Indicators, various issues.
Code: BC021

X   Components: 7 Lagging Indicators; Ratio, Constant-Dollar Inventories to Sales, Manufacturing, and Trade (%); seasonally adjusted; from January 1970.
Source: *Survey of Current Business,* Business Cycle Indicators, various issues.
Code: BC022

Y   Components: 7 Lagging Indicators; Avg. (Mean) Duration Unemployment (weeks); seasonally adjusted; from January 1970.
Source: *Survey of Current Business,* Business Cycle Indicators, various issues.
Code: BC023

Z   Components: 7 Lagging Indicators; Ratio; Consumer Installment Debt to Personal Income (%); seasonally adjusted; from January 1970.
Source: *Survey of Current Business,* Business Cycle Indicators, various issues.
Code: BC024

AA Components: 7 Lagging Indicators; Average Prime Rate Charged by Banks; %; from January 1970.
Source: *Survey of Current Business,* Business Cycle Indicators, various issues.
Code: BC025

AB Components: 7 Lagging Indicators; Commercial and Industrial Loans Outstanding; millions of 1982$; seasonally adjusted; from January 1970.
Source: *Survey of Current Business,* Business Cycle Indicators, various issues.
Code: BC026

AC Components: 7 Lagging Indicators; Change in Consumer Price Index for Services; Smoothed; seasonally adjusted; from January 1970.
Source: *Survey of Current Business,* Business Cycle Indicators, various issues.
Code: BC027

National Product and Income
Spreadsheet: NATLPROD.WK1   *Quarterly Data*

A   Year of the observation
     Code: NPYR

B   Quarter of the observation (1 = First quarter; 2 = Second quarter; etc.)
     Code: NPQU

C   National Product: Gross Domestic Product: Total; billions of dollars; seasonally adjusted; from First quarter 1959.
     Source: *Survey of Current Business,* various issues.
     Code: NP001

D   National Product: Gross Domestic Product: Personal Consumption Expenditures; total; billions of dollars; seasonally adjusted; from First quarter 1946.
     Source: *Survey of Current Business,* various issues.
     Code: NP002

E   National Product: Gross Domestic Product: Personal Consumption Expenditures; durable goods; billions of dollars; seasonally adjusted; from First quarter 1946.
     Source: *Survey of Current Business,* various issues.
     Code: NP003

F   National Product: Gross Domestic Product: Personal Consumption Expenditures; nondurable goods; billions of dollars; seasonally adjusted; from First quarter 1946.
     Source: *Survey of Current Business,* various issues.
     Code: NP004

G   National Product: Gross Domestic Product: Personal Consumption Expenditures; services; billions of dollars; seasonally adjusted; from First quarter 1946.
     Source: *Survey of Current Business,* various issues.
     Code: NP005

H   National Product: Gross Domestic Product: Gross Private Domestic Investment; total; billions of dollars; seasonally adjusted; from First quarter 1946.
     Source: *Survey of Current Business,* various issues.
     Code: NP006

I   National Product: Gross Domestic Product: Gross Private Domestic Investment; fixed investment; billions of dollars; seasonally adjusted; from First quarter 1946.
Source: *Survey of Current Business,* various issues.
Code: NP007

J   National Product: Gross Domestic Product: Gross Private Domestic Investment; fixed investment; nonresidential; billions of dollars; seasonally adjusted; from First Quarter 1946.
Source: *Survey of Current Business,* various issues.
Code: NP008

K   National Product: Gross Domestic Product: Gross Private Domestic Investment; fixed investment; residential; billions of dollars; seasonally adjusted; from First Quarter 1946.
Source: *Survey of Current Business,* various issues.
Code: NP009

L   National Product: Gross Domestic Product: Change in Business Inventories; total; billions of dollars; seasonally adjusted; from First quarter 1946.
Source: *Survey of Current Business,* various issues.
Code: NP010

M   National Product: Gross Domestic Product: Change in Business Inventories; total; billions of 1987 dollars; seasonally adjusted; from First quarter 1959.
Source: *Survey of Current Business,* various issues.
Code: NP011

N   National Product: Gross Domestic Product: Change in Business Inventories: Nonfarm; billions of dollars; seasonally adjusted; from First quarter 1946.
Source: *Survey of Current Business,* various issues.
Code: NP012

O   National Product: Gross Domestic Product: Change in Business Inventories: Farm; billions of dollars; seasonally adjusted; from First quarter 1946.
Source: *Survey of Current Business,* various issues.
Code: NP013

P   National Product: Gross Domestic Product: Net Exports of Goods and Services; total; billions of dollars; seasonally adjusted; from First quarter 1946.
Source: *Survey of Current Business,* various issues.
Code: NP014

Q National Product: Gross Domestic Product: Net Exports of Goods and Services: Exports; billions of dollars; seasonally adjusted; from First quarter 1946.
Source: *Survey of Current Business,* various issues.
Code: NP015

R National Product: Gross Domestic Product: Net Exports of Goods and Services: Imports; billions of dollars; seasonally adjusted; from First quarter 1946.
Source: *Survey of Current Business,* various issues.
Code: NP016

S National Product: Gross Domestic Product: Government Purchases of Goods and Services; total; billions of dollars; seasonally adjusted; from First quarter 1946.
Source: *Survey of Current Business,* various issues.
Code: NP017

T National Product: Gross Domestic Product: Government Purchases of Goods and Services: Federal; billions of dollars; seasonally adjusted; from First quarter 1946.
Source: *Survey of Current Business,* various issues.
Code: NP018

U National Product: Gross Domestic Product: Government Purchases of Goods and Services: Federal, National Defense; billions of dollars; seasonally adjusted; from First quarter 1946.
Source: *Survey of Current Business,* various issues.
Code: NP019

V National Product: Gross Domestic Product: Government Purchases of Goods and Services: Federal, Nondefense; billions of dollars; seasonally adjusted; from First quarter 1946.
Source: *Survey of Current Business,* various issues.
Code: NP020

W National Product: Gross Domestic Product: Government Purchases of Goods and Services: State and Local; billions of dollars; seasonally adjusted; from First quarter 1946.
Source: *Survey of Current Business,* various issues.
Code: NP021

X National Product: Gross Domestic Product: Business; Total; billions of dollars; seasonally adjusted; from First quarter 1946.
Source: *Survey of Current Business,* various issues.
Code: NP022

Y   National Product: Gross Domestic Product: Business, Nonfarm; billions of dollars; seasonally adjusted; from First quarter 1946.
Source: *Survey of Current Business,* various issues.
Code: NP023

Z   National Product: Gross Domestic Product: Business, Farm; billions of dollars; seasonally adjusted; from First quarter 1946.
Source: *Survey of Current Business,* various issues.
Code: NP024

AA   National Product: Gross Domestic Product: Households and Institutions; billions of dollars; seasonally adjusted; from First quarter 1946.
Source: *Survey of Current Business,* various issues.
Code: NP025

AB   National Product: Gross Domestic Product: Households and Institutions, Private Households; billions of dollars; seasonally adjusted; from First quarter 1946.
Source: *Survey of Current Business,* various issues.
Code: NP026

AC   National Product: Gross Domestic Product: Households and Institutions, Nonprofit Institutions; billions of dollars; seasonally adjusted; from First quarter 1946.
Source: *Survey of Current Business,* various issues.
Code: NP027

AD   National Product: Gross Domestic Product: General Government; total; billions of dollars; seasonally adjusted; from First quarter 1946.
Source: *Survey of Current Business,* various issues.
Code: NP028

AE   National Product: Gross Domestic Product: General Government, Federal; billions of dollars; seasonally adjusted; from First quarter 1946.
Source: *Survey of Current Business,* various issues.
Code: NP029

AF   National Product: Gross Domestic Product: General Government, State and Local; billions of dollars; seasonally adjusted; from First quarter 1946.
Source: *Survey of Current Business,* various issues.
Code: NP030

AG   National Product: Gross National Product; total; billions of dollars; seasonally adjusted; from First quarter 1946.
Source: *Survey of Current Business,* various issues.
Code: NP031

AH National Product: Gross National Product, Consumption of Fixed Capital; billions of dollars; seasonally adjusted; from First quarter 1946.
Source: *Survey of Current Business,* various issues.
Code: NP032

AI National Product: Net National Product; billions of dollars; seasonally adjusted; from First quarter 1946.
Source: *Survey of Current Business,* various issues.
Code: NP033

AJ National Product: Net National Product, Indirect Business Tax and Non-tax Liability; billions of dollars; seasonally adjusted; from First quarter 1946.
Source: *Survey of Current Business,* various issues.
Code: NP034

AK National Product: Net Domestic Product; total; billions of dollars; seasonally adjusted; from First quarter 1959.
Source: *Survey of Current Business,* various issues.
Code: NP035

AL National Product: Command-Basis Gross National Product; total; billions of dollars; seasonally adjusted; from First quarter 1959.
Source: *Survey of Current Business,* various issues.
Code: NP036

AM National Product: Gross Domestic Product of Corporate Business; billions of dollars; seasonally adjusted; from First quarter 1946.
Source: *Survey of Current Business,* various issues.
Code: NP037

AN National Product: Gross Domestic Product of Financial Corporate Business; billions of dollars; seasonally adjusted; from First quarter 1946.
Source: *Survey of Current Business,* various issues.
Code: NP038

AO National Product: Gross Domestic Product of Nonfinancial Corporate Business; billions of dollars; seasonally adjusted; from First quarter 1946.
Source: *Survey of Current Business,* various issues.
Code: NP039

AP National Income: total; billions of dollars; seasonally adjusted; from First quarter 1946.
Source: *Survey of Current Business,* various issues.
Code: NP040

AQ National Income: Compensation of Employees; billions of dollars; seasonally adjusted; from First quarter 1946.
Source: *Survey of Current Business,* various issues.
Code: NP041

AR National Income: Compensation of Employees; Wages and Salaries; billions of dollars; seasonally adjusted; from First quarter 1946.
Source: *Survey of Current Business,* various issues.
Code: NP042

AS National Income: Proprietors' Income with Inventory Valuation and Capital Consumption Adjustment; billions of dollars; seasonally adjusted; from First quarter 1946.
Source: *Survey of Current Business,* various issues.
Code: NP043

AT National Income: Proprietors' Income with Inventory Valuation and Capital Consumption Adjustment, Farm; billions of dollars; seasonally adjusted; from First quarter 1946.
Source: *Survey of Current Business,* various issues.
Code: NP044

AU National Income: Proprietors' Income with Inventory Valuation and Capital Consumption Adjustment, Nonfarm; billions of dollars; seasonally adjusted; from First quarter 1946.
Source: *Survey of Current Business,* various issues.
Code: NP045

AV National Income: Rental Income of Persons with Capital Consumption Adjustment; billions of dollars; seasonally adjusted; from First quarter 1946.
Source: *Survey of Current Business,* various issues.
Code: NP046

AW National Income: Corporate Profits with Inventory Valuation Adjustment and Capital Consumption Adjustment; billions of dollars; seasonally adjusted; from First quarter 1946.
Source: *Survey of Current Business,* various issues.
Code: NP047

AX National Income: Corporate Profits After Tax with Inventory Valuation Adjustment and Capital Consumption Adjustment; billions of dollars; seasonally adjusted; from First quarter 1946.
Source: *Survey of Current Business,* various issues.
Code: NP048

A   Year of the observation
     Code: PICYR

B   Quarter of the observation (1 = First quarter; 2 = Second quarter; etc.)
     Code: PICQU

C   Personal Income: Total Personal Income; billions of dollars; from First quarter
     1946.
     Source: *Survey of Current Business,* various issues.
     Code: PIC001

D   Personal Income: Wage and Salary Disbursements; billions of dollars; from
     First quarter 1946.
     Source: *Survey of Current Business,* various issues.
     Code: PIC002

E   Personal Income: Wage and Salary Disbursements: Commodity-Producing
     Industries; billions of dollars; from First quarter 1946.
     Source: *Survey of Current Business,* various issues.
     Code: PIC003

F   Personal Income: Wage and Salary Disbursements: Distributive Industries;
     billions of dollars; from First quarter 1946.
     Source: *Survey of Current Business,* various issues.
     Code: PIC004

G   Personal Income: Wage and Salary Disbursements: Service Industries; billions
     of dollars; from First quarter 1946.
     Source: *Survey of Current Business,* various issues.
     Code: PIC005

H   Personal Income: Wage and Salary Disbursements: Government and
     Government Enterprises; billions of dollars; from First quarter 1946.
     Source: *Survey of Current Business,* various issues.
     Code: PIC006

I   Personal Income: Rental Income of Persons with Capital Consumption
     Adjustment; billions of dollars; from First quarter 1946.
     Source: *Survey of Current Business,* various issues.
     Code: PIC007

J   Personal Income: Personal Dividend Income; billions of dollars; from First quarter 1946.
    Source: *Survey of Current Business,* various issues.
    Code: PIC008

K   Personal Income: Personal Interest Income; billions of dollars; from First quarter 1946.
    Source: *Survey of Current Business,* various issues.
    Code: PIC009

L   Personal Income: Transfer Payments; billions of dollars; from First quarter 1946.
    Source: *Survey of Current Business,* various issues.
    Code: PIC010

M   Personal Income: Personal Tax and Nontax Payments; billions of dollars; from First quarter 1946.
    Source: *Survey of Current Business,* various issues.
    Code: PIC011

N   Personal Income: Personal Disposable Income; billions of dollars; from First quarter 1946.
    Source: *Survey of Current Business,* various issues.
    Code: PIC012

O   Personal Income: Personal Saving; billions of dollars; from First quarter 1946.
    Source: *Survey of Current Business,* various issues.
    Code: PIC013

P   Personal Consumption Expenditures: Total; billions of dollars; from First quarter 1946.
    Source: *Survey of Current Business,* various issues.
    Code: PIC014

Q   Personal Consumption Expenditures: Durable Goods; billions of dollars; from First quarter 1946.
    Source: *Survey of Current Business,* various issues.
    Code: PIC015

R   Personal Consumption Expenditures: Nondurable Goods; billions of dollars; from First quarter 1946.
    Source: *Survey of Current Business,* various issues.
    Code: PIC016

S   Personal Consumption Expenditures: Services; billions of dollars; from First quarter 1946.
     Source: *Survey of Current Business,* various issues.
     Code: PIC017

T   Personal Consumption Expenditures: Motor Vehicles and Parts; billions of dollars; from First quarter 1946.
     Source: *Survey of Current Business,* various issues.
     Code: PIC018

U   Personal Consumption Expenditures: Furniture and Household Equipment; billions of dollars; from First quarter 1946.
     Source: *Survey of Current Business,* various issues.
     Code: PIC019

V   Personal Consumption Expenditures: Food; billions of dollars; from First quarter 1946.
     Source: *Survey of Current Business,* various issues.
     Code: PIC020

W   Personal Consumption Expenditures: Clothing and Shoes; billions of dollars; from First quarter 1946.
     Source: *Survey of Current Business,* various issues.
     Code: PIC021

X   Personal Consumption Expenditures: Gasoline and Oil; billions of dollars; from First quarter 1946.
     Source: *Survey of Current Business,* various issues.
     Code: PIC022

Y   Personal Consumption Expenditures: Fuel Oil and Coal; billions of dollars; from First quarter 1959.
     Source: *Survey of Current Business,* various issues.
     Code: PIC023

Z   Personal Consumption Expenditures: Housing; billions of dollars; from First quarter 1946.
     Source: *Survey of Current Business,* various issues.
     Code: PIC024

AA   Personal Consumption Expenditures: Household Operation; billions of dollars; from First quarter 1946.
     Source: *Survey of Current Business,* various issues.
     Code: PIC025

AB Personal Consumption Expenditures: Electricity and Gas; billions of dollars; from First quarter 1959.
Source: *Survey of Current Business,* various issues.
Code: PIC026

AC Personal Consumption Expenditures: Transportation; billions of dollars; from First quarter 1946.
Source: *Survey of Current Business,* various issues.
Code: PIC027

AD Personal Consumption Expenditures: Medical Care; billions of dollars; from First quarter 1947.
Source: *Survey of Current Business,* various issues.
Code: PIC028

Labor and Employment
Spreadsheet: EMPLOY.WK1   Monthly Data

A Year of the observation
Code: LEYR

B Month of the observation (1 = January; 2 = February; etc.)
Code: LEMO

C Labor Statistics: Total; 16 years and over; Noninstitutional Population; thousands of persons; seasonally adjusted; from January 1970.
Source: U.S. Department of Labor, Bureau of Labor Statistics, *The Employment Situation - Household Survey,* various issues.
Code: LE001

D Labor Statistics: Labor Force; thousands of persons; seasonally adjusted; from January 1970.
Source: U.S. Department of Labor, Bureau of Labor Statistics, *The Employment Situation - Household Survey,* various issues.
Code: LE002

E Labor Statistics: Total employed; thousands of persons; seasonally adjusted; from January 1970.
Source: U.S. Department of Labor, Bureau of Labor Statistics, *The Employment Situation - Household Survey,* various issues.
Code: LE003

F   Labor Statistics: Employment-Population Ratio; thousands of persons; seasonally adjusted; (Total employment as a percent of the noninstitutional population) thousands of persons; from January 1970.
   Source: U.S. Department of Labor, Bureau of Labor Statistics, *The Employment Situation - Household Survey,* various issues.
   Code: LE004

G   Labor Statistics: Unemployed; seasonally adjusted; thousands of persons; from January 1970.
   Source: U.S. Department of Labor, Bureau of Labor Statistics, *The Employment Situation - Household Survey,* various issues.
   Code: LE005

H   Labor Statistics: Unemployment Rate (Unemployment as a percent of the labor force including the resident Armed Forces); seasonally adjusted; thousands of persons; from January 1970.
   Source: U.S. Department of Labor, Bureau of Labor Statistics, *The Employment Situation - Household Survey,* various issues.
   Code: LE006

I   Labor Statistics: Labor Force, Men; seasonally adjusted; thousands of persons; from January 1970.
   Source: U.S. Department of Labor, Bureau of Labor Statistics, *The Employment Situation - Household Survey,* various issues.
   Code: LE007

J   Labor Statistics: Labor Force, Women; seasonally adjusted; thousands of persons; from January 1970.
   Source: U.S. Department of Labor, Bureau of Labor Statistics, *The Employment Situation - Household Survey,* various issues.
   Code: LE008

K   Labor Statistics: Total Employed, Men; seasonally adjusted; thousands of persons; from January 1970.
   Source: U.S. Department of Labor, Bureau of Labor Statistics, *The Employment Situation - Household Survey,* various issues.
   Code: LE009

L   Labor Statistics: Total Employed, Women; seasonally adjusted; thousands of persons; from January 1970.
   Source: U.S. Department of Labor, Bureau of Labor Statistics, *The Employment Situation - Household Survey,* various issues.
   Code: LE010

M   Labor Statistics: Unemployment Rate, Men; seasonally adjusted; thousands of persons; from January 1970.
    Source: U.S. Department of Labor, Bureau of Labor Statistics, *The Employment Situation - Household Survey,* various issues.
    Code: LE011

N   Labor Statistics: Unemployment Rate, Women; seasonally adjusted; thousands of persons; from January 1970.
    Source: U.S. Department of Labor, Bureau of Labor Statistics, *The Employment Situation - Household Survey,* various issues.
    Code: LE012

O   Employment Indicators: Leading Employment Index—With Trend Factor; seasonally adjusted; 1967=100; from January 1970.
    Source: Center For International Business Cycle Research.
    Code: LE013

P   Employment Indicators: Diffusion Index: 12 Lead Indicator Components (1-mo. span); seasonally adjusted; 1967=100; from January 1970.
    Source: Center For International Business Cycle Research.
    Code: LE014

Q   Employment Indicators: Coincident Employment Index—with Trend Factor; seasonally adjusted; 1967=100; from January 1970.
    Source: Center For International Business Cycle Research.
    Code: LE014

R   Employment Indicators: Initial Claims for Unemployment Insurance; seasonally adjusted; thousands; from January 1970.
    Source: U.S. Department of Labor, Employment Training Program, *Employment Insurance Claims - Covered Unemployment,* various issues.
    Code: LE015

S   Labor Demand: Index of Help-Wanted Advertising in Newspapers; seasonally adjusted; 1967=100; from January 1970.
    Source: The Conference Board, *Help Wanted Advertising,* various issues.
    Code: LE016

T   Labor Demand: Ratio, Help-Wanted Advertising in Newspapers to Number of Unemployed; seasonally adjusted; 1967=100; from January 1970.
    Source: The Conference Board, *Help Wanted Advertising,* various issues.
    Code: LE017

Wages and Cost of Employment
Spreadsheet: WAGES.WK1   Quarterly Data

A   Year of the observation
    Code: WCEYR

B   Quarter of the observation (1 = First quarter; 2 = Second quarter; etc.)
    Code: WCEQU

C   Employment Cost Index; Wages and Salaries; All Private Non-farm Workers;
    (1989=100); from First quarter 1976.
    Source: Bureau of Labor Statistics, *Employment Cost Index for Wages and
          Salaries,* Tables 8 & 9, various issues.
    Code: WCE001

D   Employment Cost Index; Wages and Salaries; White-Collar Workers;
    (1989=100); from First quarter 1976.
    Source: Bureau of Labor Statistics, *Employment Cost Index for Wages and
          Salaries,* Tables 8 & 9, various issues.
    Code: WCE002

E   Employment Cost Index; Wages and Salaries; Blue-Collar Workers;
    (1989=100); from First quarter 1976.
    Source: Bureau of Labor Statistics, *Employment Cost Index for Wages and
          Salaries,* Tables 8 & 9, various issues.
    Code: WCE003

F   Employment Cost Index; Wages and Salaries; Manufacturing; (1989-100); from
    First quarter 1976.
    Source: Bureau of Labor Statistics, *Employment Cost Index for Wages and
          Salaries,* Tables 8 & 9, various issues.
    Code: WCE004

G   Employment Cost Index; Wages and Salaries; Nonmanufacturing; (1989=100);
    from First quarter 1976.
    Source: Bureau of Labor Statistics, *Employment Cost Index for Wages and
          Salaries,* Tables 8 & 9, various issues.
    Code: WCE005

H   Employment Cost Index; Wages and Salaries; Union Workers; (1989=100);
    from First quarter 1976.
    Source: Bureau of Labor Statistics, *Employment Cost Index for Wages and
          Salaries,* Tables 8 & 9, various issues.
    Code: WCE006

I   Employment Cost Index; Wages and Salaries; Non-Union Workers; (1989=100); from First quarter 1976.
        Source: Bureau of Labor Statistics, *Employment Cost Index for Wages and Salaries*, Tables 8 & 9, various issues.
        Code: WCE007

J   Employment Cost Index; Compensation: Civilian Workers; (1989=100); from First quarter 1982.
        Source: Bureau of Labor Statistics, *Employment Cost Index for Wages, Salaries, and Compensation*, Table 4, various issues.
        Code: WCE008

K   Employment Cost Index; Compensation: Civilian White-Collar Workers; (1989=100); from First quarter 1982.
        Source: Bureau of Labor Statistics, *Employment Cost Index for Wages, Salaries, and Compensation*, Table 4, various issues.
        Code: WCE009

L   Employment Cost Index; Compensation: Civilian Blue-Collar Workers; (1989=100); from First quarter 1982.
        Source: Bureau of Labor Statistics, *Employment Cost Index for Wages, Salaries, and Compensation*, Table 4, various issues.
        Code: WCE010

M   Employment Cost Index; Compensation: Private Industrial Workers; (1989=100); from First quarter 1980.
        Source: Bureau of Labor Statistics, *Employment Cost Index for Wages, Salaries, and Compensation*, Table 4, various issues.
        Code: WCE011

N   Employment Cost Index; Compensation: Union Workers; (1989=100); from First quarter 1980.
        Source: Bureau of Labor Statistics, *Employment Cost Index for Private Industry Workers by Bargaining Status*, Table 6, various issues.
        Code: WCE012

O   Employment Cost Index; Compensation: Non-union Workers; (1989=100); from First quarter 1980.
        Source: Bureau of Labor Statistics, *Employment Cost Index for Private Industry Workers by Bargaining Status*, Table 6, various issues.
        Code: WCE013

P   Employment Cost Index; Benefits: Private Industry Workers (Total); (1989=100); from First quarter 1980.
      Source: Bureau of Labor Statistics, *Employment Cost Index for Wages, Salaries, and Compensation,* Table 10, various issues.
      Code: WCE014

Q   Employment Cost Index; Benefits: White-Collar Occupations; (1989=100); from First quarter 1980.
      Source: Bureau of Labor Statistics, *Employment Cost Index for Wages, Salaries, and Compensation,* Table 10, various issues.
      Code: WCE015

R   Employment Cost Index; Benefits: Blue-Collar Occupations; (1989=100); from First quarter 1980.
      Source: Bureau of Labor Statistics, *Employment Cost Index for Wages, Salaries, and Compensation,* Table 10, various issues.
      Code: WCE016

Government Receipts and Expenditures
Spreadsheet: FEDFISCL.WK1   Quarterly Data

A   Year of the observation
      Code: FISYR

B   Quarter of the observation (1 = First quarter; 2 = Second quarter; etc.)
      Code: FISQU

C   Federal Government: Receipts; billions of dollars; seasonally adjusted; from First quarter 1946.
      Source: U.S. Department of Commerce, Bureau of Economic Analysis, *Survey of Current Business,* various issues.
      Code: FIS001

D   Federal Government: Receipts: Personal Tax and Non-tax Receipts; billions of dollars; seasonally adjusted; from First quarter 1946.
      Source: U.S. Department of Commerce, Bureau of Economic Analysis, *Survey of Current Business,* various issues.
      Code: FIS002

E   Federal Government: Receipts: Personal Tax and Non-tax Receipts, Income Taxes; billions of dollars; seasonally adjusted; from First quarter 1946.
      Source: U.S. Department of Commerce, Bureau of Economic Analysis, *Survey of Current Business,* various issues.
      Code: FIS003

F   Federal Government: Receipts: Corporate Profits Tax Accruels; billions of dollars; seasonally adjusted; from First quarter 1946.
    Source: U.S. Department of Commerce, Bureau of Economic Analysis, *Survey of Current Business*, various issues.
    Code: FIS004

G   Federal Government: Receipts: Corporate Profits Tax Accruels; Federal Reserve Banks; billions of dollars; seasonally adjusted; from First quarter 1947.
    Source: U.S. Department of Commerce, Bureau of Economic Analysis, *Survey of Current Business*, various issues.
    Code: FIS005

H   Federal Government: Receipts: Indirect Business Tax and Non-tax Accruels; billions of dollars; seasonally adjusted; from First quarter 1946.
    Source: U.S. Department of Commerce, Bureau of Economic Analysis, *Survey of Current Business*, various issues.
    Code: FIS006

I   Federal Government: Receipts: Indirect Business Tax and Non-tax Accruels; Excise Taxes; billions of dollars; seasonally adjusted; from First quarter 1959.
    Source: U.S. Department of Commerce, Bureau of Economic Analysis, *Survey of Current Business*, various issues.
    Code: FIS007

J   Federal Government: Expenditures; billions of dollars; seasonally adjusted; from First quarter 1946.
    Source: U.S. Department of Commerce, Bureau of Economic Analysis, *Survey of Current Business*, various issues.
    Code: FIS008

K   Federal Government: Expenditures; Purchases of Goods and Services; billions of dollars; seasonally adjusted; from First quarter 1946.
    Source: U.S. Department of Commerce, Bureau of Economic Analysis, *Survey of Current Business*, various issues.
    Code: FIS009

L   Federal Government: Expenditures; Purchases of Goods and Services; National Defense; billions of dollars; seasonally adjusted; from First quarter 1946.
    Source: U.S. Department of Commerce, Bureau of Economic Analysis, *Survey of Current Business*, various issues.
    Code: FIS010

M Federal Government: Expenditures; Purchases of Goods and Services; Nondefense; billions of dollars; seasonally adjusted; from First quarter 1946.
Source: U.S. Department of Commerce, Bureau of Economic Analysis, *Survey of Current Business*, various issues.
Code: FIS011

N Federal Government: Expenditures; Transfer Payments (Net); billions of dollars; seasonally adjusted; from First quarter 1946.
Source: U.S. Department of Commerce, Bureau of Economic Analysis, *Survey of Current Business*, various issues.
Code: FIS012

O Federal Government: Expenditures; Grants-in-Aid to State and Local Governments; billions of dollars; seasonally adjusted; from First quarter 1946.
Source: U.S. Department of Commerce, Bureau of Economic Analysis, *Survey of Current Business*, various issues.
Code: FIS013

P Federal Government: Expenditures; Net Interest Paid; billions of dollars; seasonally adjusted; from First quarter 1946.
Source: U.S. Department of Commerce, Bureau of Economic Analysis, *Survey of Current Business*, various issues.
Code: FIS014

Q Federal Government: Expenditures; Interest Paid; billions of dollars; seasonally adjusted; from First quarter 1960.
Source: U.S. Department of Commerce, Bureau of Economic Analysis, *Survey of Current Business*, various issues.
Code: FIS015

R Federal Government: Expenditures; Interest Paid to Persons and Business; billions of dollars; seasonally adjusted; from First quarter 1960.
Source: U.S. Department of Commerce, Bureau of Economic Analysis, *Survey of Current Business*, various issues.
Code: FIS016

S Federal Government: Expenditures; Interest Paid to Foreigners; billions of dollars; seasonally adjusted; from First quarter 1960.
Source: U.S. Department of Commerce, Bureau of Economic Analysis, *Survey of Current Business*, various issues.
Code: FIS017

T   Federal Government: Surplus or Deficit (-), National Income and Product Accounts; billions of dollars; seasonally adjusted; from First quarter 1946.
Source: U.S. Department of Commerce, Bureau of Economic Analysis, *Survey of Current Business*, various issues.
Code: FIS018

U   State and Local Government: Receipts; billions of dollars; seasonally adjusted; from First quarter 1946.
Source: U.S. Department of Commerce, Bureau of Economic Analysis, *Survey of Current Business*, various issues.
Code: FIS019

V   State and Local Government: Expenditures; billions of dollars; seasonally adjusted; from First quarter 1946.
Source: U.S. Department of Commerce, Bureau of Economic Analysis, *Survey of Current Business*, various issues.
Code: FIS020

W   State and Local Government: Surplus or Deficit (-), National Income and Product Accounts; billions of dollars; seasonally adjusted; from First quarter 1946.
Source: U.S. Department of Commerce, Bureau of Economic Analysis, *Survey of Current Business*, various issues.
Code: FIS021

Production and Capacity Utilization
Spreadsheet: INDUPROD.WK1   Monthly Data

A   Year of the observation
Code: IPYR

B   Month of the observation (1 = January; 2 = February; etc.)
Code: IPMO

C   Industrial Production Indexes: Total Index; (1987=100); seasonally adjusted; from January 1970.
Source: Board of Governors of the Federal Reserve System, *Industrial Production, Statistical Release G17.*
Code: IP001

D   Industrial Production Indexes: Durable Manufactures; (1987=100); seasonally adjusted; from January 1970.
     Source: Board of Governors of the Federal Reserve System, *Industrial Production, Statistical Release G17.*
     Code: IP002

E   Industrial Production Indexes: Nondurable Manufactures; (1987=100); seasonally adjusted; from January 1970.
     Source: Board of Governors of the Federal Reserve System, *Industrial Production, Statistical Release G17.*
     Code: IP003

F   Industrial Production Indexes: Consumer Goods; (1987=100); seasonally adjusted; from January 1970.
     Source: Board of Governors of the Federal Reserve System, *Industrial Production, Statistical Release G17.*
     Code: IP004

G   Capacity Utilization: Manufacturing; (percent of capacity); seasonally adjusted; from January 1970.
     Source: Board of Governors of the Federal Reserve System, *Industrial Production and Capacity Utilization and Industrial Materials, Statistical Release G.3.*
     Code: IP005

H   Capacity Utilization: Durable Manufacturing; (percent of capacity); seasonally adjusted; from January 1970.
     Source: Board of Governors of the Federal Reserve System, *Industrial Production and Capacity Utilization and Industrial Materials, Statistical Release G.3.*
     Code: IP006

I   Capacity Utilization: Nondurable Manufacturing; (percent of capacity); seasonally adjusted; from January 1970.
     Source: Board of Governors of the Federal Reserve System, *Industrial Production and Capacity Utilization and Industrial Materials, Statistical Release G.3.*
     Code: IP007

J   Capacity Utilization: Mining; (percent of capacity); seasonally adjusted; from January 1970.
     Source: Board of Governors of the Federal Reserve System, *Industrial Production and Capacity Utilization and Industrial Materials, Statistical Release G.3.*
     Code: IP008

K   Capacity Utilization: Utilities; (percent of capacity); seasonally adjusted; from January 1970.

   Source: Board of Governors of the Federal Reserve System, *Industrial Production and Capacity Utilization and Industrial Materials, Statistical Release G.3.*

   Code: IP009

L   Index of Industrial Production; United States (1987=100); from January 1970.

   Source: U.S. Department of Commerce, The Bureau of Economic Analysis, *The Survey of Current Business,* various issues.

   Code: IP010

Foreign Industrial Production
Spreadsheet: FORPROD.WK1   Monthly Data

A   Year of the observation

   Code: FPYR

B   Month of the observation (1 = First quarter; 2 = Second quarter; etc.)

   Code: FPMO

C   Index of Industrial Production; United States (1987=100); from January 1970.

   Source: U.S. Department of Commerce, The Bureau of Economic Analysis, *The Survey of Current Business,* various issues.

   Code: FP001

D   Index of Industrial Production; OECD (1987=100); from January 1970.

   Source: U.S. Department of Commerce, The Bureau of Economic Analysis, *The Survey of Current Business,* various issues.

   Code: FP002

E   Index of Industrial Production; Japan (1987=100); from January 1970.

   Source: U.S. Department of Commerce, The Bureau of Economic Analysis, *The Survey of Current Business,* various issues.

   Code: FP003

F   Index of Industrial Production; West Germany (1987=100); from January 1970.

   Source: U.S. Department of Commerce, The Bureau of Economic Analysis, *The Survey of Current Business,* various issues.

   Code: FP004

G   Index of Industrial Production; France (1987=100); from January 1970.
      Source: U.S. Department of Commerce, The Bureau of Economic Analysis, *The Survey of Current Business*, various issues.
      Code: FP005

H   Index of Industrial Production; United Kingdom (1987=100); from January 1970.
      Source: U.S. Department of Commerce, The Bureau of Economic Analysis, *The Survey of Current Business*, various issues.
      Code: FP006

I   Index of Industrial Production; Italy (1987=100); from January 1970.
      Source: U.S. Department of Commerce, The Bureau of Economic Analysis, *The Survey of Current Business*, various issues.
      Code: FP007

J   Index of Industrial Production; Canada (1987=100); from January 1970.
      Source: U.S. Department of Commerce, The Bureau of Economic Analysis, *The Survey of Current Business*, various issues.
      Code: FP008

Key Economic Sectors

Energy
Spreadsheet: ENERGY.WK1   Monthly Data

A   Year of the observation
      Code: ENYR

B   Month of the observation (1 = January; 2 = February; etc.)
      Code: ENMO

C   Energy Consumption: Total Energy Consumption; quadrillion BTUS; seasonally adjusted; from January 1974.
      Source: U.S. Department of Energy, *Monthly Energy Review*, various issues.
      Code: EN001

D   Energy Consumption: Coal; quadrillion BTUS; seasonally adjusted; from January 1974.
      Source: U.S. Department of Energy, *Monthly Energy Review*, various issues.
      Code: EN002

E   Energy Consumption: Natural Gas (Dry); quadrillion BTUS; seasonally adjusted; from January 1974.
    Source: U.S. Department of Energy, *Monthly Energy Review*, various issues.
    Code: EN003

F   Energy Consumption: Petroleum; quadrillion BTUS; seasonally adjusted; from January 1974.
    Source: U.S. Department of Energy, *Monthly Energy Review*, various issues.
    Code: EN004

G   Petroleum Production: Total Petroleum Products Supplied; thousands of barrels per day; from January 1974.
    Source: U.S. Department of Energy, *Monthly Energy Review*, various issues.
    Code: EN005

H   Crude Oil - Refiners' Costs: Composite, dollars per barrel; from January 1974.
    Source: U.S. Department of Energy, *Monthly Energy Review*, various issues.
    Code: EN006

I   Gasoline Prices: U.S. City Average: Retail, all types of gasoline; cents per gallon; from January 1978.
    Source: U.S. Department of Labor, Bureau of Labor Statistics, *Consumer Prices*, various issues.
    Code: EN007

J   Price Index of U.S. Crude Petroleum Imports from: All Countries, (1977=100); from January 1976.
    Source: U.S. Department of Labor, Bureau of Labor Statistics, Division of International Prices, *Price Indexes of U.S. Crude Petroleum Imports by Source*, various issues.
    Code: EN008

K   Price Index of U.S. Crude Petroleum Imports from: OPEC Countries, (1977=100); from January 1976.
    Source: U.S. Department of Labor, Bureau of Labor Statistics, Division of International Prices, *Price Indexes of U.S. Crude Petroleum Imports by Source*, various issues.
    Code: EN009

Housing and Construction
Spreadsheet: HOUSING.WK1   Monthly Data

A   Year of the observation
     Code: HOUSYR

B   Month of the observation (1 = January; 2 = February; etc.)
     Code: HOUSMO

C   Housing Starts: New Privately Owned Housing Units Started; total; (Nonfarm + Farm); thousands of units; seasonally adjusted; from January 1970.
     Source: U.S. Department of Commerce, Bureau of the Census, *Housing Starts and Building Permits*, (Monthly News Release), various issues.
     Code: HOUS001

D   Housing Starts: Total Private Housing Units Started; thousands of units; seasonally adjusted; from January 1970.
     Source: U.S. Department of Commerce, Bureau of the Census, *Housing Starts and Building Permits*, (Monthly News Release), various issues.
     Code: HOUS002

E   Housing Starts: Index of New Private Housing Authorized by Local Building Permits; (1967=100); seasonally adjusted; from January 1970.
     Source: U.S. Department of Commerce, Bureau of Economic Analysis, *Survey of Current Business*, various issues.
     Code: HOUS003

F   Housing: New Privately Owned Housing Units Completed; total; thousands of units; seasonally adjusted; from January 1970.
     Source: U.S. Department of Commerce, Bureau of the Census, *Housing Completions*, various issues.
     Code: HOUS004

G   Housing: New Privately Owned Housing Units Under Construction; total; thousands of units; seasonally adjusted; from January 1970.
     Source: U.S. Department of Commerce, Bureau of the Census, *Housing Completions*, various issues.
     Code: HOUS005

H   Construction: Value of New Construction; Total Private and Public Construction; millions of dollars; seasonally adjusted; from January 1970.
     Source: U.S. Department of Commerce, Bureau of the Census, *Value of New Construction Put in Place, Construction Reports*, various issues.
     Code: HOUS006

I   Construction: Value of New Construction, Private Residential Buildings; millions of dollars; seasonally adjusted; from January 1970.
    Source: U.S. Department of Commerce, Bureau of the Census, *Value of New Construction Put in Place, Construction Reports*, various issues.
    Code: HOUS007

J   Construction: Value of New Construction, Commercial and Industrial Buildings; millions of dollars; seasonally adjusted; from January 1970.
    Source: U.S. Department of Commerce, Bureau of the Census, *Value of New Construction Put in Place, Construction Reports*, various issues.
    Code: HOUS008

K   Construction: Value of New Construction, Public Construction; millions of dollars; seasonally adjusted; from January 1970.
    Source: U.S. Department of Commerce, Bureau of the Census, *Value of New Construction Put in Place, Construction Reports*, various issues.
    Code: HOUS009

L   Construction Indexes: Bureau of the Census Composite Fixed-Weight Price Index; (1987=100); seasonally adjusted; from January 1970.
    Source: U.S. Department of Commerce, Bureau of the Census, *Value of New Construction Put in Place, Construction Reports*, various issues.
    Code: HOUS010

M   Construction Indexes: Bureau of the Census Implicit Price Deflator; (1987=100); seasonally adjusted; from January 1970.
    Source: U.S. Department of Commerce, Bureau of the Census, *Value of New Construction Put in Place, Construction Reports*, various issues.
    Code: HOUS011

Automotive
Spreadsheet: AUTOS.WK1 Monthly Data

A   Year of the observation
     Code: AUTOYR

B   Month of the observation (1 = January; 2 = February; etc.)
     Code: AUTOMO

C   Domestic Trade: Retail Sales: Automotive Dealers; seasonally adjusted; millions of dollars; from January 1970.
     Source: U.S. Department of Commerce, Bureau of the Census, Current Business Reports:, *Monthly Retail Sales and Inventories, Manufacturing and Trade: Inventories and Sales*, various issues.
     Code: AUTO001

D   Domestic Trade: Retail Inventories: Automotive Dealers; seasonally adjusted; millions of dollars; from January 1970.
     Source: U.S. Department of Commerce, Bureau of the Census, Current Business Reports:, *Monthly Retail Sales and Inventories, Manufacturing and Trade: Inventories and Sales*, various issues.
     Code: AUTO002

E   Retail Automobile and Truck Sales: Total New Passenger Cars, millions of units; seasonally adjusted; millions of dollars; from January 1970.
     Source: U.S. Department of Commerce, Bureau of Economic Analysis, *Survey of Current Business*, various issues.
     Code: AUTO003

F   Retail Automobile and Truck Sales: Domestic New Passenger Cars; millions of units; seasonally adjusted; millions of dollars; from January 1970.
     Source: U.S. Department of Commerce, Bureau of Economic Analysis, *Survey of Current Business*, various issues.
     Code: AUTO004

G   Retail Automobile and Truck Sales: Foreign New Passenger Cars; millions of units; seasonally adjusted; millions of dollars; from January 1970.
     Source: U.S. Department of Commerce, Bureau of Economic Analysis, *Survey of Current Business*, various issues.
     Code: AUTO005

H   Inventory/Sales Ratio: New Passenger Car Units, Domestic; seasonally adjusted; from January 1970.
    Source: U.S. Department of Commerce, Bureau of Economic Analysis, Unpublished Printout: *Automobile Sales and Inventories,*
    Code: AUTO006

I   Average Expenditure per Car, Overall; ($/car) seasonally adjusted; from January 1970.
    Source: U.S. Department of Commerce, Bureau of Economic Analysis, Unpublished Printout: *Automobile Sales and Inventories,*
    Code: AUTO007

J   Average Expenditure per Car, Overall, Domestic; ($/car) seasonally adjusted; from January 1970.
    Source: U.S. Department of Commerce, Bureau of Economic Analysis, Unpublished Printout: *Automobile Sales and Inventories,*
    Code: AUTO008

K   Average Expenditure per Car, Overall, Foreign; ($/car) seasonally adjusted; from January 1970.
    Source: U.S. Department of Commerce, Bureau of Economic Analysis, Unpublished Printout: *Automobile Sales and Inventories,*
    Code: AUTO009

Manufacturing
Spreadsheet: MANUFAC.WK1   Monthly Data

A   Year of the observation
    Code: MANYR

B   Quarter of the observation (1 = First quarter; 2 = Second quarter; etc.)
    Code: MANMO

C   Manufacturing and Trade: Business Cycle Indicators, Sales; billions of dollars, seasonally adjusted; from January 1970.
    Source: U.S. Department of Commerce, Bureau of Economic Analysis, *Survey of Current Business*, various issues.
    Code: MAN001

D   Manufacturing and Trade: Business Cycle Indicators, Inventories (Book Value); billions of dollars; seasonally adjusted; from January 1970.
    Source: U.S. Department of Commerce, Bureau of Economic Analysis, *Survey of Current Business*, various issues.
    Code: MAN002

E Manufacturing and Trade: Business Cycle Indicators, Change in Inventories (Book Value); billions of dollars; seasonally adjusted; from January 1970.
  Source: U.S. Department of Commerce, Bureau of Economic Analysis, *Survey of Current Business*, various issues.
  Code: MAN003

F Manufacturing and Trade: Inventories and Sales in Real Dollars, Inventories (end of month); Manufacturing; billions of 1982 dollars; seasonally adjusted; from January 1970.
  Source: U.S. Department of Commerce, Bureau of Economic Analysis, Unpublished Printout.
  Code: MAN004

G Manufacturing and Trade: Inventories and Sales in Real Dollars, Inventories (end of month); Merchant Wholesalers; billions of 1982 dollars; seasonally adjusted; from January 1970.
  Source: U.S. Department of Commerce, Bureau of Economic Analysis, Unpublished Printout.
  Code: MAN005

H Manufacturing and Trade: Inventories and Sales in Real Dollars, Inventories (end of month); Retail Trade; billions of 1982 dollars; seasonally adjusted; from January 1970.
  Source: U.S. Department of Commerce, Bureau of Economic Analysis, Unpublished Printout.
  Code: MAN006

I Manufacturing and Trade: Inventories and Sales in Real Dollars, Sales (end of month); Manufacturing; billions of 1982 dollars; seasonally adjusted; from January 1970.
  Source: U.S. Department of Commerce, Bureau of Economic Analysis, Unpublished Printout.
  Code: MAN007

J Manufacturing and Trade: Inventories and Sales in Real Dollars, Sales (end of month); Merchant Wholesalers; billions of 1982 dollars; seasonally adjusted; from January 1970.
  Source: U.S. Department of Commerce, Bureau of Economic Analysis, Unpublished Printout.
  Code: MAN008

K   Manufacturing and Trade: Inventories and Sales in Real Dollars, Sales (end of month); Retail Trade; billions of 1982 dollars; seasonally adjusted; from January 1970.
     Source: U.S. Department of Commerce, Bureau of Economic Analysis, Unpublished Printout.
     Code: MAN009

L   Manufacturing: Manufacturers' Shipments: Total Manufacturing Industries; millions of dollars; seasonally adjusted; from January 1970.
     Source: U.S. Department of Commerce, Bureau of Economic Analysis, *Current Industrial Reports, Manufacturers' Shipments, Inventories, and Orders,* various issues.
     Code: MAN010

M   Manufacturing: Inventories (end of month): Total Manufacturing Inventories; millions of dollars; seasonally adjusted; from January 1970.
     Source: U.S. Department of Commerce, Bureau of Economic Analysis, *Current Industrial Reports, Manufacturers' Shipments, Inventories, and Orders,* various issues.
     Code: MAN011

N   Manufacturing: New Orders: Total Manufacturing Inventories; millions of dollars; seasonally adjusted; from January 1970.
     Source: U.S. Department of Commerce, Bureau of Economic Analysis, *Current Industrial Reports, Manufacturers' Shipments, Inventories, and Orders,* various issues.
     Code: MAN012

O   Manufacturing: Unfilled Orders (end of month): Total Manufacturing Inventories; millions of dollars; seasonally adjusted; from January 1970.
     Source: U.S. Department of Commerce, Bureau of Economic Analysis, *Current Industrial Reports, Manufacturers' Shipments, Inventories, and Orders,* various issues.
     Code: MAN013

Corporations

Corporate Profits
Spreadsheet: CORPPROF.WK1   Quarterly Data

A   Year of the observation
     Code: CPROFYR

B   Quarter of the observation (1 = First quarter; 2 = Second quarter; etc.)
     Code: CPROFQU

C   Corporate Profits with Inventory Valuation & Capital Consumption Adjustments; total; billions of dollars; seasonally adjusted; from First quarter 1946.
     Source: U.S. Department of Commerce, Bureau of Economic Analysis; *The National Income and Product Accounts of the United States, & The Survey of Current Business*, various issues.
     Code: CPROF001

D   Corporate Profits with Inventory Valuation & Capital Consumption Adjustments; Domestic Industries; billions of dollars; seasonally adjusted; from First quarter 1946.
     Source: U.S. Department of Commerce, Bureau of Economic Analysis; *The National Income and Product Accounts of the United States, & The Survey of Current Business*, various issues.
     Code: CPROF002

E   Corporate Profits with Inventory Valuation & Capital Consumption Adjustments; Domestic Industries, Financial; billions of dollars; seasonally adjusted; from First quarter 1946.
     Source: U.S. Department of Commerce, Bureau of Economic Analysis; *The National Income and Product Accounts of the United States, & The Survey of Current Business*, various issues.
     Code: CPROF003

F   Corporate Profits with Inventory Valuation & Capital Consumption Adjustments; Domestic Industries, Nonfinancial; billions of dollars; seasonally adjusted; from First quarter 1946.
     Source: U.S. Department of Commerce, Bureau of Economic Analysis; *The National Income and Product Accounts of the United States, & The Survey of Current Business*, various issues.
     Code: CPROF004

G Corporate Profits with Inventory Valuation; Financial Institutions (excluding Federal Reserve Banks); billions of dollars; seasonally adjusted; from First quarter 1946.

  Source: U.S. Department of Commerce, Bureau of Economic Analysis; *The National Income and Product Accounts of the United States, & The Survey of Current Business*, various issues.

  Code: CPROF005

H Corporate Profits with Inventory Valuation; Manufacturing; billions of dollars; seasonally adjusted; from First quarter 1946.

  Source: U.S. Department of Commerce, Bureau of Economic Analysis; *The National Income and Product Accounts of the United States, & The Survey of Current Business*, various issues.

  Code: CPROF006

I Corporate Profits with Inventory Valuation; Manufacturing, Durable Goods; billions of dollars; seasonally adjusted; from First quarter 1946.

  Source: U.S. Department of Commerce, Bureau of Economic Analysis; *The National Income and Product Accounts of the United States, & The Survey of Current Business*, various issues.

  Code: CPROF007

J Corporate Profits with Inventory Valuation; Manufacturing, Nondurable Goods; billions of dollars; seasonally adjusted; from First quarter 1946.

  Source: U.S. Department of Commerce, Bureau of Economic Analysis; *The National Income and Product Accounts of the United States, & The Survey of Current Business*, various issues.

  Code: CPROF008

K Corporate Profits with Inventory Valuation; Transportation and Public Utilities; billions of dollars; seasonally adjusted; from First quarter 1946.

  Source: U.S. Department of Commerce, Bureau of Economic Analysis; *The National Income and Product Accounts of the United States, & The Survey of Current Business*, various issues.

  Code: CPROF009

L Corporate Profits with Inventory Valuation; Wholesale and Retail Trade; billions of dollars; seasonally adjusted; from First quarter 1946.

  Source: U.S. Department of Commerce, Bureau of Economic Analysis; *The National Income and Product Accounts of the United States, & The Survey of Current Business*, various issues.

  Code: CPROF010

M   Corporate Profits with Inventory Valuation; Mining; billions of dollars; seasonally adjusted; from First quarter 1946.
     Source: U.S. Department of Commerce, Bureau of Economic Analysis, Unpublished Data.
     Code: CPROF011

N   Corporate Profits with Inventory Valuation; Construction; billions of dollars; seasonally adjusted; from First quarter 1946.
     Source: U.S. Department of Commerce, Bureau of Economic Analysis, Unpublished Data.
     Code: CPROF012

O   Corporate Profits with Inventory Valuation; Transportation; billions of dollars; seasonally adjusted; from First quarter 1946.
     Source: U.S. Department of Commerce, Bureau of Economic Analysis, Unpublished Data.
     Code: CPROF013

P   Corporate Profits with Inventory Valuation; Communication; billions of dollars; seasonally adjusted; from First quarter 1946.
     Source: U.S. Department of Commerce, Bureau of Economic Analysis, Unpublished Data.
     Code: CPROF014

Q   Corporate Profits with Inventory Valuation; Electricity, Gas, and Sanitary Services; billions of dollars; seasonally adjusted; from First quarter 1946.
     Source: U.S. Department of Commerce, Bureau of Economic Analysis, Unpublished Data.
     Code: CPROF015

R   Corporate Profits with Inventory Valuation; Finance, Insurance, and Real Estate; billions of dollars; seasonally adjusted; from First quarter 1946.
     Source: U.S. Department of Commerce, Bureau of Economic Analysis, Unpublished Data.
     Code: CPROF016

S   Corporate Profits with Inventory Valuation; Services; billions of dollars; seasonally adjusted; from First quarter 1946.
     Source: U.S. Department of Commerce, Bureau of Economic Analysis, Unpublished Data.
     Code: CPROF017

Fixed Capital Investment
Spreadsheet: FXINVEST.WK1 Quarterly Data

A   Year of the observation
    Code: FCIYR

B   Quarter of the observation (1 = First quarter; 2 = Second quarter; etc.)
    Code: FCIQU

C   Fixed Capital Investment; Nonresidential; billions of dollars; seasonally adjusted; from First quarter 1946.
    Source: U.S. Department of Commerce, Bureau of Economic Analysis, *The Survey of Current Business,* various issues.
    Code: FCI001

D   Fixed Capital Investment; Nonresidential, Structures; billions of dollars; seasonally adjusted; from First quarter 1946.
    Source: U.S. Department of Commerce, Bureau of Economic Analysis, *The Survey of Current Business,* various issues.
    Code: FCI002

E   Fixed Capital Investment; Producers Durable Equipment; billions of dollars; seasonally adjusted; from First quarter 1946.
    Source: U.S. Department of Commerce, Bureau of Economic Analysis, *The Survey of Current Business,* various issues.
    Code: FCI003

F   Fixed Capital Investment; Producers Durable Equipment, Information Processing and Related Equipment; billions of dollars; seasonally adjusted; from First quarter 1947.
    Source: U.S. Department of Commerce, Bureau of Economic Analysis, *The Survey of Current Business,* various issues.
    Code: FCI004

G   Fixed Capital Investment; Industrial Equipment; billions of dollars; seasonally adjusted; from First quarter 1947.
    Source: U.S. Department of Commerce, Bureau of Economic Analysis, *The Survey of Current Business,* various issues.
    Code: FCI005

H   Fixed Capital Investment; Nonresidential Buildings, Excluding Farm; millions of dollars; from First quarter 1958.
    Source: U.S. Department of Commerce, Bureau of Economic Analysis, Unpublished Data.
    Code: FCI006

I   Fixed Capital Investment; Nonresidential Buildings, Excluding Farm, Industrial; millions of dollars; from First quarter 1959.
     Source: U.S. Department of Commerce, Bureau of Economic Analysis, Unpublished Data.
     Code: FCI007

J   Fixed Capital Investment; Nonresidential Buildings, Excluding Farm, Commercial, millions of dollars; from First quarter 1959.
     Source: U.S. Department of Commerce, Bureau of Economic Analysis, Unpublished Data.
     Code: FCI008

K   Fixed Capital Investment; Utilities, millions of dollars; from First quarter 1959.
     Source: U.S. Department of Commerce, Bureau of Economic Analysis, Unpublished Data.
     Code: FCI009

L   Fixed Capital Investment; Utilities, Railroads; millions of dollars; from First quarter 1959.
     Source: U.S. Department of Commerce, Bureau of Economic Analysis, Unpublished Data.
     Code: FCI010

M   Fixed Capital Investment; Utilities, Telecommunications; millions of dollars; from First quarter 1959.
     Source: U.S. Department of Commerce, Bureau of Economic Analysis, Unpublished Data.
     Code: FCI011

N   Business Investment Expenditures; Wholesale and Retail Trade; billions of dollars; seasonally adjusted; from First quarter 1947.
     Source: U.S. Department of Commerce, Bureau of Economic Analysis, *Survey of Current Business*.
     Code: FCI012

O   Business Investment Expenditures; Finance and Insurance; billions of dollars; seasonally adjusted; from First quarter 1947.
     Source: U.S. Department of Commerce, Bureau of Economic Analysis, *Survey of Current Business*.
     Code: FCI013

P   Business Investment Expenditures; Personal and Business Services; billions of dollars; seasonally adjusted; from First quarter 1947.
     Source: U.S. Department of Commerce, Bureau of Economic Analysis, *Survey of Current Business*.
     Code: FCI014

Q   Business Investment Expenditures; Communication; billions of dollars; seasonally adjusted; from First quarter 1947.
Source: U.S. Department of Commerce, Bureau of Economic Analysis, *Survey of Current Business.*
Code: FCI015

Business Inventories
Spreadsheet: INVENTOR.WK1   Quarterly Data

A   Year of the observation
Code: INVYR

B   Quarter of the observation (1 = First quarter; 2 = Second quarter; etc.)
Code: INVQU

C   Change in Business Inventories: Total; billions of dollars; from First quarter 1946.
Source: U.S. Department of Commerce, Bureau of Economic Analysis, *Survey of Current Business,* various issues.
Code: INV001

D   Change in Business Inventories: Total; Nonfarm, billions of dollars; from First quarter 1946.
Source: U.S. Department of Commerce, Bureau of Economic Analysis, *Survey of Current Business,* various issues.
Code: INV002

E   Change in Business Inventories: Manufacturing; billions of dollars; from First quarter 1946.
Source: U.S. Department of Commerce, Bureau of Economic Analysis, *Survey of Current Business,* various issues.
Code: INV003

F   Change in Business Inventories: Wholesale Trade; billions of dollars; from First quarter 1946.
Source: U.S. Department of Commerce, Bureau of Economic Analysis, *Survey of Current Business,* various issues.
Code: INV004

G   Change in Business Inventories: Retail Trade; billions of dollars; from First quarter 1946.
Source: U.S. Department of Commerce, Bureau of Economic Analysis, *Survey of Current Business,* various issues.
Code: INV005

H   Inventories (End of Quarter): Total; billions of dollars; from 4th quarter 1947.
     Source: U.S. Department of Commerce, Bureau of Economic Analysis, *Survey of Current Business,* various issues.
     Code: INV006

I   Inventories (End of Quarter): Total, Nonfarm; billions of dollars; from 4th quarter 1947.
     Source: U.S. Department of Commerce, Bureau of Economic Analysis, *Survey of Current Business,* various issues.
     Code: INV007

J   Inventories (End of Quarter): Manufacturing; billions of dollars; from 4th quarter 1947.
     Source: U.S. Department of Commerce, Bureau of Economic Analysis, *Survey of Current Business,* various issues.
     Code: INV008

K   Inventories (End of Quarter): Wholesale Trade; billions of dollars; from 4th quarter 1947.
     Source: U.S. Department of Commerce, Bureau of Economic Analysis, *Survey of Current Business,* various issues.
     Code: INV009

L   Inventories (End of Quarter): Retail Trade; billions of dollars; from 4th quarter 1947.
     Source: U.S. Department of Commerce, Bureau of Economic Analysis, *Survey of Current Business,* various issues.
     Code: INV010

Commodity Prices

Commodity Price Indexes
Spreadsheet: COMPRICE.WK1   Monthly Data

A   Year of the observation
    Code: COMYR

B   Month of the observation (1 = January; 2 = February; etc.)
    Code: COMMO

C   Commodity Research Bureau Spot Market Index: All Commodities; (1967=100); from January 1970.
    Source: Commodity Research Bureau, Inc., *CRB Commodity Index Report*, various issues.
    Code: COM001

D   Commodity Research Bureau Spot Market Index: Foodstuffs; (1967=100); from January 1970.
    Source: Commodity Research Bureau, Inc., *CRB Commodity Index Report*, various issues.
    Code: COM002

E   Commodity Research Bureau Spot Market Index: Raw Industrials; (1967=100); from January 1970.
    Source: Commodity Research Bureau, Inc., *CRB Commodity Index Report*, various issues.
    Code: COM003

F   Index of Prices Received by Farmers for All Farm Products; (1977=100); from January 1970.
    Source: U.S. Department of Agriculture, Crop Reporting Board, Statistical Reporting Service, *Agricultural Prices*, various issues.
    Code: COM004

G   Industrial Materials Price Index; (1985=100); from January 1970.
    Source: *Journal of Commerce*, various issues.
    Code: COM005

International Trade

Balance of Trade Statistics
Spreadsheet: TRADEBAL.WK1 Monthly Data

A   Year of the observation
     Code: INTYR

B   Month of the observation (1 = January; 2 = February; etc.)
     Code: INTMO

C   Exports, Domestic and Foreign Merchandise (Free Alongside Ship); millions
     of dollars; seasonally adjusted; from January 1984.
     Source: U.S. Department of Commerce, Bureau of the Census, *Summary of*
          U.S. Export-Import Merchandise Trade, various issues.
     Code: INT001

D   General Imports of Merchandise (Custom's Value); millions of dollars;
     seasonally adjusted; from January 1986.
     Source: U.S. Department of Commerce, Bureau of the Census, *Summary of*
          U.S. Export-Import Merchandise Trade, various issues.
     Code: INT002

E   Trade Balance: F.A.S. Exports; Customs Imports; millions of dollars; seasonally
     adjusted; from January 1986.
     Source: U.S. Department of Commerce, Bureau of the Census, *Summary of*
          U.S. Export-Import Merchandise Trade, various issues.
     Code: INT003

F   Total Exports: Food, Beverages, and Tobacco (F.A.S.); millions of dollars; from
     January 1970.
     Source: U.S. Department of Commerce, Bureau of the Census, *Summary of*
          U.S. Export-Import Merchandise Trade, various issues.
     Code: INT004

G   Total Exports: Crude Materials and Fuels (Including Fats and Oils), (F.A.S.);
     millions of dollars; from January 1970.
     Source: U.S. Department of Commerce, Bureau of the Census, *Summary of*
          U.S. Export-Import Merchandise Trade, various issues.
     Code: INT005

H   Total Exports: Manufactured Goods, (F.A.S.); millions of dollars; from January 1970.
     Source: U.S. Department of Commerce, Bureau of the Census, *Summary of U.S. Export-Import Merchandise Trade,* various issues.
     Code: INT006

I   Total Imports: Food, Beverage, and Tobacco, [F.A.S. (77-81), Customs Value, (81-Present)]; millions of dollars; from January 1970.
     Source: U.S. Department of Commerce, Bureau of the Census, *Summary of U.S. Export-Import Merchandise Trade,* various issues.
     Code: INT007

J   Total Imports: Crude Materials and Fuels (Including Fats and Oils), [F.A.S. (77-81), Customs Value, (81-Present)]; millions of dollars; from January 1970.
     Source: U.S. Department of Commerce, Bureau of the Census, *Summary of U.S. Export-Import Merchandise Trade,* various issues.
     Code: INT008

K   Total Imports: Manufactured Goods, [F.A.S. (77-81), Customs Value, (81-Present)]; millions of dollars; from January 1970.
     Source: U.S. Department of Commerce, Bureau of the Census, *Summary of U.S. Export-Import Merchandise Trade,* various issues.
     Code: INT009

L   U.S. Trade Balance (Exports less Imports): Canada; millions of dollars; from January 1974.
     Source: U.S. Department of Commerce, Bureau of the Census, *Summary of U.S. Export-Import Merchandise Trade,* various issues.
     Code: INT010

M   U.S. Trade Balance (Exports less Imports): United Kingdom; millions of dollars; from January 1974.
     Source: U.S. Department of Commerce, Bureau of the Census, *Summary of U.S. Export-Import Merchandise Trade,* various issues.
     Code: INT011

N   U.S. Trade Balance (Exports less Imports): Federal Republic of Germany; millions of dollars; from January 1974.
     Source: U.S. Department of Commerce, Bureau of the Census, *Summary of U.S. Export-Import Merchandise Trade,* various issues.
     Code: INT012

O   U.S. Trade Balance (Exports less Imports): France; millions of dollars; from January 1974.
Source: U.S. Department of Commerce, Bureau of the Census, *Summary of U.S. Export-Import Merchandise Trade,* various issues.
Code: INT013

P   U.S. Trade Balance (Exports less Imports): Italy; millions of dollars; from January 1974.
Source: U.S. Department of Commerce, Bureau of the Census, *Summary of U.S. Export-Import Merchandise Trade,* various issues.
Code: INT014

Q   U.S. Trade Balance (Exports less Imports): Japan; millions of dollars; from January 1974.
Source: U.S. Department of Commerce, Bureau of the Census, *Summary of U.S. Export-Import Merchandise Trade,* various issues.
Code: INT015

4
Exercises

Exercise 1
Measures of the Money Supply

Contributed by Brian S. Wilson
Spreadsheet: MONEYSUP.WK1

Compute the percentage change of each component for the periods shown in the table below.

Growth in the Money Supply From 1970–1992				
Period	Percentage Growth in M1	Percentage Growth in M2	Percentage Growth in M3	Percentage Growth in L
Jan 1970–Dec 1974				
Jan 1975–Dec 1979				
Jan 1980–Dec 1984				
Jan 1985–Mar 1989				
Jan 1970–Mar 1992				

According to M1, during which of the four periods did the money supply expand the most? Which measure of the money supply has experienced the highest growth from January 1970 to March 1992? What are the components that make up this measure?

Prepare a line graph that illustrates each of the money supply measures (M1, M2, M3, and L) from January 1970 through March 1992. (Let the X-axis run from 1970 to 1992, and set the Y-axis to run from 0 to 6000.)

Exercise 2
Money in the U.S. Economy

Contributed by Ricardo J. Rodriguez
Spreadsheet: MONEYSUP.WK1

Find the correlation coefficient between each pair of money measures and complete the correlation matrix shown below.

Correlation Matrix for the Various Definitions of Money			
	M1	**M2**	**M3**	**L**
M1	1.00			
M2		1.00		
M3			1.00	
L				1.00

Based on the completed table, to what extent is one money measure a substitute for the other? Given the degree of correlation you have found, is there really any need for more than one of these indexes? Explain.

Exercise 3
Components of M2

Contributed by Brian S. Wilson
Spreadsheet: MONEYSUP.WK1

Complete the following table and prepare a pie graph showing the components of M2 for December 1990. (Do not divide M1 into components.)

Components of M2		
Component	**Billions of Dollars**	**% of M2**
M1		
Overnight Repurchase Agreements		
Overnight Eurodollars		
Money Market Mutual Fund Balances		
Savings Deposits		
Small Denomination Time Deposits		

Which component makes up the largest proportion of M2? How can the Federal Reserve exert control over this component?

Exercise 4
Currency and Demand Deposits

Contributed by Ricardo J. Rodriguez
Spreadsheet: MONEYSUP.WK1

The classical theory of money creation assumes that the ratio of currency in circulation to demand deposits is a constant, c.

During which periods has the ratio of currency to demand deposits been approximately constant? Compute the average and the standard deviation of the c-ratio over the entire period, as well as for each available complete decade, and complete the table below.

Ratio of Currency in Circulation to Demand Deposits		
Period	Average	Standard Deviation
1970s		
1980s		
1970–1992		

Prepare a graph that shows the evolution of this ratio for 1970–1992. (Let the X-axis run from 1970/1 to 1992/7, and set the Y-axis to run from .2 to 1.)

Exercise 5
Overnight Repurchase Agreements
and Overnight Eurodollars

Contributed by Ricardo J. Rodriguez
Spreadsheet: MONEYSUP.WK1

Prepare a graph showing the evolution of very short-term financing through the use of overnight repurchase agreements and through overnight Eurodollars for 1977–1992. (Let the X-axis run from 1977/1 to 1992/7, and set the Y-axis to run from $0 to $80 billion.)

Using linear regression over the entire period for each instrument, predict the use of these two financing sources in the year 2000. To perform the regression, create a time index by letting January 1977 be t = 1, February 1977 be t = 2, and so on. Then regress the column containing the repo data against the newly created index column. Do the same for the column containing the Eurodollar data. Based on the past growth patterns, how reliable do you think these projections are?

What can you conclude about the relative importance of each of these instruments in the near future?

Exercise 6
The Evolution of Commercial Paper

Contributed by Ricardo J. Rodriguez
Spreadsheet: MONEYSUP.WK1

Prepare a graph showing the evolution of the level of commercial paper for 1970–1992. (Let the X-axis run from 1970/1 to 1992/6, and set the Y-axis to run from $0 to $400 billion.)

Using linear regression over the entire period, predict the use of this source of financing in the year 2000. To perform the regression, create a time index by letting January 1970 be t = 1, February 1970 be t = 2, and so on. Then regress the column containing the commercial paper data against the newly created index column. Based on the past growth pattern of commercial paper, how reliable do you think this projection is?

Exercise 7
The Velocity of Money (M3)

Contributed by Brian S. Wilson
Spreadsheets: FINQU.WK1, NATLPROD.WK1

The average number of times a unit of money is used in one period is called the velocity of money. This is computed by dividing the GNP by a measure of the money supply. Prepare a line graph depicting the velocity of money from quarter 1 in 1960 through quarter 4 of 1990. Use M3 as the money supply measure. Based on your visual analysis of the graph, how has the velocity of money changed throughout this period? What economic variables would influence the velocity of money?

Exercise 8
Money Velocity

Contributed by Ricardo J. Rodriguez
Spreadsheets: FINQU.WK1, NATLPROD.WK1

The velocity of money is defined as the ratio of the gross national product (GNP) to the money stock. Since there are four major definitions of money, there are also four measures of velocity.

Compute the average velocity for each complete decade and for each of the four definitions of money, and complete the table shown below.

Average Velocity of Money				
Period	M1 Velocity	M2 Velocity	M3 Velocity	L Velocity
1960s				
1970s				
1980s				
1970–1992				

What major characteristics of each of these velocity measures stand out? Which has been the most stable measure of velocity?

Prepare a graph showing the evolution of the M1 and M2 velocity of money for 1970–1992. (Let the X-axis run from 1959/1Q to 1992/2Q, and set the Y-axis to run from 1 to 8.)

Exercise 9
The Money Multiplier

Contributed by Ricardo J. Rodriguez
Spreadsheets: MONEYSUP.WK1, RESERVES.WK1

The money multiplier is defined as the ratio of the money stock to the monetary base. Compute the average money multiplier for each complete decade and complete the table shown below.

The Money Multiplier for M1 and M2		
Period	M1 Multiplier	M2 Multiplier
1970s		
1980s		
1970–1992		

Which of these two measures has been more stable?

Prepare a graph showing the evolution of the money multiplier for 1970–1992. Use only M1 and M2 as the measure of money. (Let the X-axis run from 1970/1 to 1992/7, and set the Y-axis to run from 2 to 14.)

Exercise 10
Vault Cash as a Percentage
of Demand Deposits

Contributed by Ricardo J. Rodriguez
Spreadsheets: RESERVES.WK1, MONEYSUP.WK1

Consider the ratio of vault cash to demand deposits for 1970 through July 1992. Find the average and standard deviation for this ratio to complete the table shown below.

Ratio of Vault Cash to Demand Deposits		
Period	**Average**	**Standard Deviation**
1970s		
1980s		
1970–1992		

Prepare a graph showing the evolution of the ratio of vault cash to demand deposits for 1970–1992. (Let the X-axis run from 1970/1 to 1992/7, and set the Y-axis to run from 2 to 13 percent.) Describe the main characteristics of this graph. Does the graph suggest any peculiar behavior in this ratio?

Exercise 11
The Excess Reserves Ratio

Contributed by Ricardo J. Rodriguez
Spreadsheets: MONEYSUP.WK1, RESERVES.WK1

It is usually argued that banks hold very few of their assets in the form of excess reserves. The excess reserves ratio, e, is defined as the ratio of excess reserves to demand deposits. Consider the period from January 1970 through July 1992. Find the average excess reserves ratio for each complete decade and for the entire period. In similar fashion find the standard deviation for the same periods, as well as the coefficient of variation (standard deviation/average), and complete the table shown below.

The Excess Reserves Ratio			
Period	Average	Standard Deviation	Coefficient of Variation
1970s			
1980s			
1970–1992			

Do the data in the table support the idea that the excess reserves ratio is low and stable?

Prepare a graph showing the evolution of the excess reserves ratio for 1970–1992. (Let the X-axis run from 1970/1 to 1992/7, and set the Y-axis to run from 0 to .009.)

Exercise 12
Excess Reserves and
the Fed Funds Rate

Contributed by Brian S. Wilson
Spreadsheets: MONEYSUP.WK1, RESERVES.WK1, MONEYYLD.WK1

Prepare a graph that compares the amount of excess reserves held by banks and the federal funds rate from January 1970 to December 1991 and complete the following table.

(HINT: Present the amount of excess reserves as a ratio to demand deposits. Excess reserves must be converted to billions. To make the graph comparable, set each series so that January of 1970 equals 100).

Excess Reserves and the Fed Funds Rate		
Period	Average Fed Funds Rate	Average Ratio of Excess Reserves to Demand Deposits
Jan 1970–Dec 1974		
Jan 1975–Dec 1979		
Jan 1980–Dec 1984		
Jan 1985–Dec 1989		
Jan 1990–Dec 1991		

Based on a visual inspection of the graph, do you see any correlation between the Federal Funds Rate and Excess Reserves? What other factors would influence the amount of Excess Reserves held by banks?

Exercise 13
The Required Reserves Ratio

Contributed by Ricardo J. Rodriguez
Spreadsheets: MONEYSUP.WK1, RESERVES.WK1

In many textbook models, the average required reserves ratio is defined as the ratio of required reserves to demand deposits. Prepare a graph showing the evolution of this required reserves ratio for 1970–1992. (Let the X-axis run from 1970/1 to 1992/7, and set the Y-axis to run from .07 to .17.)

Find the mean of the average required reserves ratio for each complete decade and for the entire period. In similar fashion find the standard deviation and the coefficient of variation (standard deviation/average) for the same periods and complete the table shown below.

The Required Reserves Ratio			
Period	Average	Standard Deviation	Coefficient of Variation
1970s			
1980s			
1970–1992			

Does the data suggest any substantial change in the required reserve ratio through time?

Exercise 14
M1 and Inflation

Contributed by Brian S. Wilson
Spreadsheets: MONEYSUP.WK1, INFLATE.WK1

For 1980 to 1991, compute the annual percentage change of M1 and the annual percentage change in the CPI. Complete the following table and prepare a line graph depicting the CPI and M1 from January 1970 through July 1992. To make the series comparable, set the M1 value for June of 1983 equal to a base of 100. Does growth in inflation appear to be correlated with growth in M1?

Changes in M1 and Inflation		
Period	Percent Change in M1	Percent Change in CPI
Jan–Dec 1980		
Jan–Dec 1981		
Jan–Dec 1982		
Jan–Dec 1983		
Jan–Dec 1984		
Jan–Dec 1985		
Jan–Dec 1986		
Jan–Dec 1987		
Jan–Dec 1988		
Jan–Dec 1989		
Jan–Dec 1990		
Jan–Dec 1991		

Exercise 15
The Distribution of Inflation

Contributed by Ricardo J. Rodriguez
Spreadsheet: INFLATE.WK1

Prepare a graph showing the evolution of monthly inflation for all items in the U.S. for 1970–1992. (Let the X-axis run from February 1970 to July 1992, and set the Y-axis to run from -1 percent to 2 percent.). Also make a histogram of the distribution of monthly inflation by counting the number of months for which inflation fell within a certain range, and complete the table shown below.

The Distribution of Monthly Inflation		
Range (Percent)	**Number of Months in the Range**	**Percentage of Months in the Range**
-.6 to -.4		
-.4 to -.2		
-.2 to 0		
0 to .2		
.2 to .4		
.4 to .6		
.6 to .8		
.8 to 1		
1 to 1.2		
1.2 to 1.4		
1.4 to 1.6		
1.6 to 1.8		
1.8 to 2.0		

Describe the major characteristics of this distribution. What is the average inflation? What is the standard deviation of the distribution of inflation? Is the distribution skewed?

Exercise 16
Measures of Inflation

Contributed by Brian S. Wilson
Spreadsheets: FINQU.WK1, INFLATE.WK1

Complete the following table showing the CPI, PPI, and GNP deflator. For the CPI and PPI, use values from December for the year indicated. For the GNP deflator use values from the fourth quarter for the year indicated.

Measures of Inflation			
Year	CPI Index: All Items (1982–1984 = 100)	PPI Index: All Commodities (1982–1984 = 100)	GNP Deflator (1987 = 100)
1970			
1975			
1980			
1985			
1990			
Average Annual Inflation Rate			

By which measure has inflation increased the most from 1970 to 1990? Which measure contains the widest group of goods?

Exercise 17
The Correlation Among
Various Consumer Price Indexes

Contributed by Ricardo J. Rodriguez
Spreadsheet: INFLATE.WK1

Find the correlation coefficient among the consumer price indexes for food and beverages, housing, and services, for January 1970 to July 1992, and complete the correlation matrix shown below.

Correlation Matrix for the Consumer Price Indexes			
	CPI Food & Beverages	CPI Housing	CPI Services
CPI Food & Beverages	1.00		
CPI Housing		1.00	
CPI Services			1.00

Based on the completed table, to what extent is one index a substitute for the other? Given the degree of correlation you have found, is there really any need for more than one of these indexes? Explain.

Exercise 18
Inflation in the United States and Japan

Contributed by Robert W. Kolb
Spreadsheet: FORINFLA.WK1

Complete the following table for inflation in the selected countries:

Percentage Change in Consumer Price Index		
Country	January 1970 to December 1979	January 1980 to December 1989
United States		
Japan		
Germany		
United Kingdom		
Italy		
Canada		

What was the annualized rate of inflation in the United States and Japan for the decade of the 1980s (more specifically, the 118 month period from January 1980 to December 1989)?

Prepare a graph showing inflation in the United States and Japan from January 1970 through December 1991. (Let the X-axis run from 1970 to 1991, and set the Y-axis to run from 0 to 160.)

Exercise 19
Worldwide Correlations in Inflation

Contributed by Robert W. Kolb
Spreadsheet: FORINFLA.WK1

For the United States, Japan, Germany, and the United Kingdom, compute the monthly percentage change in the consumer price index for the period from February 1970 through the end of 1991. Using these percentage changes, compute the correlations in inflation among these four countries. Complete the table below by entering the correlations.

Correlation Matrix for Inflation Rates				
	U.S.	Japan	Germany	U.K.
U.S.	1.0			
Japan		1.0		
Germany			1.0	
U.K.				1.0

Based on the completed table, to what extent is inflation a common phenomenon around the world? Is there really any tendency for the major economic powers to experience inflation simultaneously?

Using the percentage changes that you computed, find the month of the highest and lowest inflation for each country. Complete the table below by indicating the percentage change that was the highest and lowest for each country in this period.

Highest and Lowest Monthly Inflation for Four Countries, 1970–1991				
	U.S.	Japan	Germany	U.K.
Highest value				
Lowest value				

Did any country experience deflation at any time? Explain.

Exercise 20
Banks and Consumer Credit

Contributed by Robert W. Kolb
Spreadsheet: CONSUMCR.WK1

For the period from January 1975 through the end of 1989, prepare a graph showing the percentage of total consumer installment credit outstanding that was financed at commercial banks. (Let the X-axis run from 1975 to 1989, and set the Y-axis to run from .4 to .55.) How has this changed over time? Can you explain why it might have changed as indicated?

For December 1980 and December 1989, complete the following table that shows the amounts of revolving credit held by banks, retailers, and gasoline companies.

Holding of Revolving Consumer Credit, 1980 and 1989 Millions of Dollars				
	Banks	**Retailers**	**Gasoline Companies**	**Total**
December 1980				
December 1989				

How can you explain the differences that have arisen in the relative holdings of these three kinds of providers of credit?

Exercise 21
Mutual Fund Indexes

Contributed by Robert W. Kolb
Spreadsheet: LIPPER.WK1

For the period January 1987 through December 1991, compute the mean monthly growth in the mutual fund indexes and the standard deviation for the indexes shown in the table below. Do these values correspond to the risk levels implied by the type of fund? Explain.

Mutual Fund Index Performance		
Fund Index	Mean Monthly Growth	Standard Deviation
Balanced		
Growth and Income		
Growth		
Small Company Growth		

Exercise 22
The Correlations Among
Various Mutual Fund Indexes

Contributed by Ricardo J. Rodriguez
Spreadsheet: LIPPER.WK1

Find the correlation coefficient between the Lipper mutual fund indexes for capital appreciation, growth, and gold, for 1986/12 to 1992/9, and complete the correlation matrix shown below.

Correlation Matrix for the Lipper Mutual Fund Indexes			
	Capital Appreciation	Growth	Gold
Capital Appreciation	1.00		
Growth		1.00	
Gold			1.00

Based on the completed table, to what extent is one index a substitute for the other? Given the degree of correlation you have found, is there really any need for more than one of these indexes? Explain.

Exercise 23
Net Asset Values of Fidelity Funds

Contributed by Ricardo J. Rodriguez
Spreadsheet: MUTUFUND.WK1

Prepare a graph that shows the net asset values (NAV) for Fidelity's capital appreciation fund, growth and income fund, high yield fund, and the Magellan fund for 1987–1992. To compare the relative performances of each index, create separate indexes for each of the funds as follows. Set the first observation (January 1987) of the capital appreciation fund so that it is equal to 1, by dividing it by itself. All other observations of this fund should also be divided by the first observation. Set the first observation of the growth and income fund to 2. For the high yield fund, set the first observation to 3, and for the Magellan fund, set it to 4. (Let the X-axis run from 1987/1 to 1992/9, and set the Y-axis to run from 0 to 6.)

Find the correlation coefficient between each pair of money measures and complete the correlation matrix shown below.

Correlation for Net Asset Values of Selected Fidelity Mutual Funds				
	Capital Appreciation	**Growth and Income**	**High Yield**	**Magellan**
Capital Appreciation	1.00			
Growth and Income		1.00		
High Yield			1.00	
Magellan				1.00

Based on the completed table, to what extent is one mutual fund a substitute for the other? Given the degree of correlation you have found, is there really any need to invest in more than one of these mutual funds?

Exercise 24
Stock and Bond Issues

Contributed by Robert W. Kolb
Spreadsheet: PRIMMKT.WK1

Do U.S. corporations raise more funds by issuing stock or by selling bonds? For the period from January 1970 through December 1991, prepare a graph showing the ratio of funds raised by offering of bonds as a percentage of any new security issues. (Let the X-axis run from 1970 to 1991, and set the Y-axis to run from .2 to 1.0.)

What do these results say about the relative importance of debt and equity in the financing of U.S. corporations? Comment on any extended trends that you observe in this proportion.

Exercise 25
Correlations Among Stock Indexes

Contributed by Robert W. Kolb
Spreadsheet: STKINDEX.WK1

For the Dow Jones Industrial Averages (DJIA), the New York Stock Exchange Composite Index (NYSE), and the S&P 500 index, compute the monthly percentage change in the consumer price index for the period from February 1970 through the end of 1991. Using these percentage changes, compute the correlations among these three indexes. Complete the table below by entering the correlations.

Correlation Matrix for Major Stock Indexes			
	DJIA	NYSE	S&P 500
DJIA	1.0		
NYSE		1.0	
S&P 500			1.0

Based on the completed table, to what extent is one index a substitute for another? Given the degree of correlation that you have found, is there really any need for more than one of these indexes? Explain.

Complete the table below by indicating the percentage change that was the highest and lowest for each index in this period.

Highest and Lowest Monthly Returns for Three Indexes, 1970–1991			
	DJIA	NYSE	S&P 500
Highest value			
Lowest value			

Exercise 26
The Betas of Various Indexes
Relative to the S&P 500 Index

Contributed by Ricardo J. Rodriguez
Spreadsheet: STKINDEX.WK1

Using the Standard and Poor's composite index of 500 stocks (the S&P 500) as a proxy for the market, calculate the beta of the Dow Jones industrial average of 30 stocks, of the New York stock exchange composite index, and of the S&P 500 index itself. Present the results of your calculation in the table below. You will need to prepare new columns for each of these variables that represent the monthly return for each of the indexes. In the process, the initial observation will be lost. Compute a single beta for each index using data from 1970 to 1992.

The Beta of Various Indexes	
Index	**Beta**
DJIA 30	
NYSE Composite	
S&P 500	

The beta of any asset j can be calculated by performing the following regression:

$$R_{j,t} = \alpha_j + \beta_j R_{m,t} + \varepsilon_t$$

where:

$R_{j,t}$ = return on asset j in period t
$R_{m,t}$ = return on market portfolio in period t

Do these betas conform to your expectations?

Exercise 27
The Betas of Various Indexes Relative to the New York Stock Exchange Composite Index

Contributed by Ricardo J. Rodriguez
Spreadsheet: STKINDEX.WK1

Using the New York stock exchange composite index as a proxy for the market, calculate the beta of the Dow Jones industrial average of 30 stocks, of the New York stock exchange composite index itself, and of the S&P 500 index. Present the results of your calculation in the table below. You will need to prepare new columns for each of these variables that represent the monthly return for each of the indexes. In the process, the initial observation will be lost. Compute a single beta for each index using data from 1970 to 1992.

The Beta of Various Indexes	
Index	Beta
DJIA 30	
NYSE Composite	
S&P 500	

The beta of any asset j can be calculated by performing the following regression:

$$R_{j,t} = \alpha_j + \beta_j R_{m,t} + \varepsilon_t$$

where:

$R_{j,t}$ = return on asset j in period t
$R_{m,t}$ = return on market portfolio in period t

Do these betas conform to your expectations?

Exercise 28
Serial Correlation in Equity Returns

Contributed by Robert W. Kolb
Spreadsheet: STKINDEX.WK1

For the period from February 1970 to December 1991, compute the percentage change in the NYSE Composite Index (DELTANY). Regress the percentage change on the percentage change from the previous period, running the following regression:

$$\text{DELTANY}_t = \alpha + \beta\text{DELTANY}_{t-1} + \varepsilon_t$$

(Setting up this regression results in the loss of two observations. January 1970 is lost to form the return from January to February, and another observation is lost because of lagging by one period.) Based on the regression results, complete the following table.

Results from Regressing the Percentage Change of the NYSE Composite on its Lagged Values, 1970 to 1991			
	α	β	R^2
$\text{DELTANY}_t = \alpha + \beta\text{DELTANY}_{t-1} + \varepsilon_t$			

What do these regression results show about the tendency of stock market increases in one month to be followed by increases in the next month? To what extent is this result consistent with any version of the efficient markets hypothesis? Explain.

Using the same observations from the regression, prepare a graph that records DELTANY^t on the vertical axis and DELTANY^{t-1} on the X-axis. (Let the X-axis run from -.15 to .15, and set the Y-axis to run from -.15 to .15. Use the XY graph type, and show only symbols, not lines.) What does the graph reveal about the relationship of stock returns in one period relative to the next period?

Exercise 29
Serial Correlation in Stock Market Levels

Contributed by Robert W. Kolb
Spreadsheet: STKINDEX.WK1

For the period from March 1970 to December 1991, regress the level of the NYSE composite index (NY) on the level of the index in the preceding period, running the following regression:

$$NY_t - \alpha + \beta NY_{t-1} + \varepsilon_t$$

Based on the regression results, complete the following table.

Results from Regressing the Level of the NYSE Composite on its Lagged Values, 1970 to 1991			
	α	β	R^2
$NY_t = \alpha + \beta NY_{t-1} + \varepsilon_t$			

What do these regression results show about the tendency of stock market levels in one month to be followed by a higher level in the next month? To what extent is this result consistent with any version of the efficient markets hypothesis? Does it shed any light on the efficient markets hypothesis? Explain. How can you interpret the large R^2 from this regression?

Using the same observations from the regression, prepare a graph that records NY^t on the vertical axis and NY^{t-1} on the horizontal axis. (Let the X–axis run from 0 to 220, and set the Y–axis to run from 0 to 220. Use the XY graph type, and show only symbols, not lines.) What does the graph reveal about the relationship of stock prices in one period relative to the next period?

Exercise 30
The Distribution of
S&P 500 Monthly Returns

Contributed by Ricardo J. Rodriguez
Spreadsheet: STKINDEX.WK1

Make a histogram of the distribution of monthly returns for the S&P 500 composite index by counting the number of months for which returns fell within a certain range and completing the table shown below. Do this for the period 1970–1992. There are 270 monthly returns.

The Distribution of Monthly Returns for the S&P 500 Index		
Range (Percent)	Number of Months in the Range	Percentage of Months in the Range
-16 to -14		
-14 to -12		
-12 to -10		
-10 to -8		
-8 to -6		
-6 to -4		
-4 to -2		
-2 to 0		
0 to 2		
2 to 4		
4 to 6		
6 to 8		
8 to 10		
10 to 12		
12 to 14		
14 to 16		

Describe the major characteristics of this distribution. What is the average monthly return? What is the standard deviation of the distribution of returns? Is the distribution skewed?

Exercise 31
Corporate Profits and Stock Prices

Contributed by Brian S. Wilson
Spreadsheets: FINQU.WK1, NATLPROD.WK1

Prepare a line graph running from the first quarter of 1947 through the fourth quarter of 1991 depicting the ratio of the New York Stock Exchange Composite stock index to corporate profits before taxes. Then complete the table below:

Corporate Profits and Stock Prices	
Period	Average Ratio of the New York Stock Exchange Composite Index to Corporate Profits Before Taxes
1st Quarter 1947–4th Quarter 1949	
1st Quarter 1950–4th Quarter 1959	
1st Quarter 1960–4th Quarter 1969	
1st Quarter 1970–4th Quarter 1979	
1st Quarter 1980–4th Quarter 1989	
1st Quarter 1990–4th Quarter 1991	

How has this relationship changed over time? In which period do stocks seem most depressed in comparison to corporate profits? In which period do stocks seem most inflated?

Exercise 32
Dividend Yield

Contributed by Robert W. Kolb
Spreadsheet: STKINDEX.WK1

For January 1970 through the end of 1991, prepare a graph showing the dividend yield on the stocks in the S&P 500 common stock index. (Let the X-axis run from .2 to .7, and set the Y-axis to run from 1970 to 1991.) Find the average of all of these months, along with the month that had the highest and the lowest values. Use these figures to complete the following table.

S&P 500 Dividend Yield, 1970 to 1991	
Average of all months	
Highest month and yield for that month	
Lowest month and yield for that month	

Find the months of the biggest increase and the greatest drop in the dividend yield over the period from February 1970 through the end of 1991. Use these values to complete the following table. Were there any special market events that could explain these large changes? Explain.

S&P 500 Dividend Yield, 1970 to 1991	
Month of largest increase and amount of the increase	
Month of largest decrease and amount of the decrease	

Exercise 33
The Stock Market Crash of October 1987

Contributed by Brian S. Wilson
Spreadsheets: STKINDEX.WK1, STOCKS.WK1

Complete the following table depicting the effects of the stock market crash of October 1987 on the various mutual funds, stock indexes, and individual stocks shown. Set each of the values of the components listed to a base in which December of 1986 equals 100. Prepare 2 line graphs, the first containing the first five stock index components, and the second containing the last four individual stock components from December of 1986 through June of 1988. Do not include the Russell 2000 in either of your graphs.

The Stock Market Crash of October 1987			
Equity Market Component	**Price or Index Value September 1987**	**Price or Index Value October 1987**	**Percent Change**
DJIA			
NYSE Composite			
NYSE Industrial			
S&P 500			
NASDAQ Composite			
Russell 2000			
IBM			
General Motors			
Ryder System			
UAL			

Which stock or stock index value was most affected? Which stock or stock index was least affected?

Exercise 34
The January Effect

Contributed by Ricardo J. Rodriguez
Spreadsheets: STKINDEX.WK1

It is said that returns in January are the highest of any month. This is the so-called January effect. Prepare a bar graph that shows the average return for each month of the year over the period from January 1970 through July 1992. Use the S&P 500 index to create a column of monthly returns for the market, and use those returns to test for the January effect. (Let the X-axis run from January to December, and set the Y-axis to run from -.02 to .04.)

To do the calculations you will need to make a table of 12 columns, one for each month of the year. From the column containing each monthly return for the S&P 500, extract all the January returns, and put them in the January column of the newly created table. Do the same for February to December. Use the S&P 500 in a conditional (IF) statement to determine the month corresponding to each return. Be careful to note that some months have 22 observations and others have 23 observations. Once you have all the returns for each month in their corresponding column, and you have determined the number of observations for each month, using another 12 column table similar to the one for returns, you can determine the average return for each month. Fill in the following table to assist you in preparing the graph.

Do your data support the January effect hypothesis?

Average Monthly Returns for the S&P 500	
Month	Average Return
January	
February	
March	
April	
May	
June	
July	
August	
September	
October	
November	
December	

Exercise 35
The Nominal and Deflated S&P 500 Index

Contributed by Ricardo J. Rodriguez
Spreadsheets: STKINDEX.WK1 and INFLATE.WK1

Prepare a graph showing the evolution of the nominal and real value of the Standard and Poor's 500 composite index for 1970–1992. Use the consumer price index for all items to deflate the nominal S&P 500 index. (Let the X-axis run from 1970/1 to 1992/7, and set the Y-axis to run from 0 to 400.)

What noteworthy characteristics are apparent in the graph?

Exercise 36
Stock Exchange Activity

Contributed by Robert W. Kolb
Spreadsheet: STKACTIV.WK1

For the period from January 1977 to December 1991, prepare a graph showing the total market value of stocks sold on all registered exchanges. (Let the X-axis run from 1977 to 1991, and set the Y-axis to run from 0 to 300.) Based on a visual inspection of the graph you created, when was the approximate period of greatest increase in activity, as measured by market value? Explain.

Prepare a second graph for the same period showing the market value activity of the New York Stock Exchange as a percentage of the total. (Let the X-axis run from 1977 to 1991, and set the Y-axis to run from .8 to .92.) How has this changed? What accounts for the relative stability or instability of this ratio?

Exercise 37
Growth in NYSE and NASDAQ Markets

Contributed by Robert W. Kolb
Spreadsheet: STKACTIV.WK1

For each month in the period from January 1983 to December 1991, find the combined market value of sales on the New York Stock Exchange and the NASDAQ. Prepare a graph showing how the percentage of this total traded on the NASDAQ has changed over this period. (Let the X-axis run from 1983 to 1991, and set the Y-axis to run from 0 to .4.) Does the graph show a substantial trend? If so, what does it suggest about the future of organized exchanges like the NYSE relative to markets with a structure like the NASDAQ?

Exercise 38
Stock Market Volume Characteristics

Contributed by Robert W. Kolb
Spreadsheet: STKACTIV.WK1

For the New York Stock Exchange during the period from January 1974 through December 1991, prepare a graph showing the percentage of NYSE volume that was traded in lots of 5,000 shares or larger. (Let the X-axis run from 1974 to 1991, and set the Y-axis to run from 0 to 80.) How has this changed over time? What do the results of your graph imply for the role of the individual shareholder as a major force in the stock market?

Exercise 39
Foreign Stock Returns

Contributed by Robert W. Kolb
Spreadsheet: FORSTOCK.WK1

For the period from January 1970 to December 1991, create a stock index that has a value of 1.0 for January 1970 for the stock indexes of the United States, Japan, Germany, and the United Kingdom. (For each country, divide all of the observations by the value of the index for January 1970.)

Based on the adjusted index that you have created, complete the following table. Do the values in this table reflect the total growth in the investment of $1 in each country's index? Explain. What does the table say about the relative performance of each country's stock market? Explain.

Adjusted Stock Index Values, December 1991				
	U.S.	Japan	Germany	U.K.
December 1991				

Exercise 40
Correlations Among
National Stock Market Returns

Contributed by Robert W. Kolb
Spreadsheet: FORSTOCK.WK1

For the period from February 1970 to December 1991, compute the percentage change in the stock indexes of the United States, Japan, Germany, and the United Kingdom. Compute the correlations in returns among these indexes, and use these values to complete the following correlation matrix.

Correlation Matrix for National Stock Market Returns, 1970 to 1991				
	U.S.	Japan	Germany	U.K.
U.S.	1.0			
Japan		1.0		
Germany			1.0	
U.K.				1.0

What do these correlations reveal about the prospects for reducing the risk of equity portfolios by investing outside one's home country? Which one country appears to offer the best diversification potential for an investor from Germany? Explain. Which pair of countries has the highest correlation? Can you explain why this might be the case?

Exercise 41
Riskiness of National
Stock Market Returns

Contributed by Robert W. Kolb
Spreadsheet: FORSTOCK.WK1

For the period from February 1970 to December 1991, compute the percentage change in the stock indexes of the United States, Japan, Germany, and the United Kingdom. Compute the mean monthly returns and standard deviation of monthly returns for each index, and use those values to complete the following table. (These returns series are used in other exercises.)

Statistics for National Stock Market Returns, 1970 to 1991				
	U.S.	Japan	Germany	U.K.
Mean Monthly Returns				
Standard Deviation				

Exercise 42
Riskiness of Two–Country
Stock Portfolios

Contributed by Robert W. Kolb
Spreadsheet: FORSTOCK.WK1

For the period from February 1970 to December 1991, compute the percentage change in the stock indexes of the United States, Japan, Germany, and the United Kingdom. Compute the mean monthly returns and standard deviation of monthly returns for each index. Using the return series just computed, create returns series for two-country internationally diversified portfolios assuming equal division of investment between two countries for the country pairs shown in the table below and compute the statistics to complete the table. (These returns series are used in other exercises.)

Statistics for Two–Country Portfolios, 1970 to 1991		
	Mean Monthly Return	**Standard Deviation**
U.S./Japan		
U.S./Germany		
U.S./U.K.		
Japan/Germany		
Japan/U.K.		
Germany/U.K.		

Create a graph showing each portfolio in risk/return space. (Let the X-axis run from 0 to .02, and set the Y-axis to run from 0 to .01. Use the XY graph type, and show only symbols, not lines.)

Exercise 43
Riskiness of Internationally Diversified Stock Portfolios

Contributed by Robert W. Kolb
Spreadsheet: FORSTOCK.WK1

For the period from February 1970 to December 1991, compute the percentage change in the stock indexes of the United States, Japan, Germany, and the United Kingdom. Compute the mean monthly returns and standard deviation of monthly returns for each index. Using the return series just computed, create returns series for three-country internationally diversified portfolios assuming equal division of investment among the three countries shown in the table below and compute the statistics to complete the table. Also, make the same computations for the four-country portfolio. (These returns series are used in other exercises.)

Statistics for International Portfolios, 1970 to 1991		
	Mean Monthly Return	**Standard Deviation**
U.S./Japan/Germany		
U.S./Germany/U.K.		
U.S./U.K./Japan		
Japan/Germany/U.K.		
All Countries		

Exercise 44
The Stock Market Crash of October 1987:
Effect on Foreign Stocks

Contributed by Brian S. Wilson
Spreadsheet: FORSTOCK.WK1

Complete the following table depicting the effects of the stock market crash of October 1987 on the stock indexes of foreign countries.

Stock Price Index	Price or Index Value September 1987	Price or Index Value October 1987	Percent Change
United States			
Japan			
Federal Republic of Germany			
France			
United Kingdom			
Italy			
Canada			
Morgan Stanley EAFE Index			

Do these index values provide evidence that the crash was felt worldwide? How does the EAFE compare with the index of the United States?

Exercise 45
Common Stock Returns

Contributed by Robert W. Kolb
Spreadsheet: STOCKS.WK1

For January 1987 through December 1991, compute monthly returns for the stocks shown in the table and complete the table. Be sure to include dividends, if any. (The returns computed here are used in other exercises.)

Common Stock Risk and Return		
Stock	Average Monthly Return	Standard Deviation
Apple Computer		
FPL Group		
Homestake Mining		
Westinghouse Electric		

Exercise 46
Real and Nominal Returns on Stocks

Contributed by Brian S. Wilson
Spreadsheets: INFLATE.WK1, STOCKS.WK1, MONEYYLD.WK1

Complete the following table by computing the annual real and nominal returns on Ryder System and Minnesota Mining and Manufacturing. Also include the January yield on a 3-month U.S. Treasury bill for the given year.

	Real and Nominal Returns on Stocks					
Year	Ryder System		Minnesota Mining and Manufacturing		3-month U.S. Treasury Bills	
	Nominal Return	Real Return	Nominal Return	Real Return	Nominal Return	Real Return
1987						
1988						
1989						
1990						
1991						

Which of these two companies managed a higher real return in 1991? In which years were the real returns on 3-month T-bills higher than those of either company?

Exercise 47
Computing Betas

Contributed by Robert W. Kolb
Spreadsheets: STOCKS.WK1, STKINDEX.WK1

Based on returns for January 1987 through December 1991, compute the beta of each stock using the market model regression formula and complete the table shown below. Use the S&P 500 index as a proxy for the market portfolio.

The market model regression equation is:

$$R_{j,t} = \alpha_j + \beta_j R_{m,t} + \varepsilon_t$$

where:

$R_{j,t}$ = return on stock j in period t
$R_{m,t}$ = return on market portfolio in period t

Common Stock Betas			
Stock	α	β	R^2
Apple Computer			
FPL Group			
Homestake Mining			
Westinghouse Electric			

Comment on the results in the table. Are the R^2s higher or lower than expected? Based on these results, which firm behaves most like the market? Which is the most aggressive?

Exercise 48
The Beta of the Risk-free Asset

Contributed by Ricardo J. Rodriguez
Spreadsheets: STKINDEX.WK1, MONEYYLD.WK1

One of the basic assumptions of the Capital Asset Pricing Model is that the returns on the market are uncorrelated with the risk-free rate. This implies that the risk-free rate should have a beta of zero. Nevertheless, both the return on the market and the risk-free rate vary through time. Therefore, it is possible to find some correlation between the two rates, in which case the beta of the risk-free rate could be statistically different from zero.

Using the 3-month Treasury bill rate as a proxy for the risk-free rate, and the return on the S&P 500 index (you need to calculate it from the price series), calculate the risk-free beta and present the results in the table below. To determine whether the beta coefficient is statistically significant, calculate its t-statistic (the ratio of the X coefficient to the standard error of the coefficient. Both of these values are part of the standard regression output). Normally, if the t-statistic has an absolute value greater than 1.96, we say that the coefficient is statistically different from zero at the 5 percent level.

The Beta of 3-month T-bills		
Period	Beta	t-statistic
1970s		
1980s		
1970–1992		

The beta of any asset j can be calculated by performing the following regression:

$$R_{j,t} = \alpha_j + \beta_j R_{m,t} + \varepsilon_t$$

where:

$R_{j,t}$ = return on asset j in period t
$R_{m,t}$ = return on market portfolio in period t

Do these results conform to the CAPM?

Exercise 49
The Beta of Energy Companies

Contributed by Ricardo J. Rodriguez
Spreadsheets: STOCKS.WK1, STKINDEX.WK1

Using the Standard and Poor's composite index of 500 stocks (the S&P 500) as a proxy for the market, calculate the beta for Chevron, Exxon, Texaco, and for a portfolio of the three equally weighted stocks. Present the results of your calculation in the table below. You will need to prepare new columns for each of these variables that represent the monthly return for each of the stocks. This requires including both the price and the dividend series for each stock. In the process, the initial observation will be lost. Compute a single beta for each stock or portfolio using data from 1986/12 to 1992/7.

The Beta of Various Energy Stocks and Portfolios	
Stock	**Beta**
Chevron	
Exxon	
Texaco	
Equally-weighted Portfolio	

The beta of any asset j can be calculated by performing the following regression:

$$R_{j,t} = \alpha_j + \beta_j R_{m,t} + \varepsilon_t$$

where:

$R_{j,t}$ = return on asset j in period t
$R_{m,t}$ = return on market portfolio in period t

Do these betas conform to your expectations?

Exercise 50
The Beta of Food and Beverage Stocks

Contributed by Ricardo J. Rodriguez
Spreadsheets: STKINDEX.WK1, STOCKS.WK1

Using the Standard and Poor's composite index of 500 stocks (the S&P 500) as a proxy for the market, calculate the beta for Anheuser Busch, Coca-Cola, McDonald's, and Pepsi-Cola. Present the results of your calculation in the table below. You will need to prepare new columns for each of these variables that represent the monthly return for each of the stocks. This requires including both the price and the dividend series for each stock. In the process, the initial observation will be lost. Compute a single beta for each stock or portfolio using data from 1986/12 to 1992/7.

The Beta of Various Food Stocks and Portfolios	
Stock	**Beta**
Anheuser Busch	
Coca-Cola	
McDonald's	
Pepsi-Cola	

The beta of any asset j can be calculated by performing the following regression:

$$R_{j,t} = \alpha_j + \beta_j R_{m,t} + \varepsilon_t$$

where:

$R_{j,t}$ = return on asset j in period t
$R_{m,t}$ = return on market portfolio in period t

Do these betas conform to your expectations?

Exercise 51
The Beta of Computer Stocks

Contributed by Ricardo J. Rodriguez
Spreadsheets: STKINDEX.WK1, STOCKS.WK1

Using the Standard and Poor's composite index of 500 stocks (the S&P 500) as a proxy for the market, calculate the beta for Apple, Hewlett-Packard, Microsoft, IBM, and Novell. Present the results of your calculation in the table below. You will need to prepare new columns for each of these variables that represent the monthly return for each of the stocks. This requires including both the price and the dividend series for each stock. In the process, the initial observation will be lost. Compute a single beta for each stock or portfolio using data from 1986/12 to 1992/7.

The Beta of Various Computer Stocks and Portfolios	
Stock	**Beta**
Apple	
Hewlett-Packard	
Microsoft	
IBM	

The beta of any asset j can be calculated by performing the following regression:

$$R_{j,t} = \alpha_j + \beta_j R_{m,t} + \varepsilon_t$$

where:

$R_{j,t}$ = return on asset j in period t
$R_{m,t}$ = return on market portfolio in period t

Do these betas conform to your expectations?

Exercise 52
Varying Volatilities Among Stocks in Different Industries

Contributed by Brian S. Wilson
Spreadsheets: STOCKS.WK1, STKINDEX.WK1

Complete the table below depicting the volatilities of stocks in various industries: Measure volatility by computing the annual coefficient of variation (standard deviation as a percent of the mean) of the closing price of each month.

Volatilities Among Stocks in Different Industries					
Period	DJIA	FPL Group Inc.	Genentech	American Telephone and Telegraph	Microsoft Corp.
1987					
1988					
1989					
1990					
1991					

Which company has the most volatile stock price in a single year? Which company has the least volatile in a single year? Do you think stock price volatility is somewhat related to the type of industry of the company?

Exercise 53
Two-Stock Portfolios

Contributed by Robert W. Kolb
Spreadsheet: STOCKS.WK1

Based on returns for January 1987 through December 1991, compute the correlation of monthly returns for the stocks shown in the table and complete the table. Be sure to include dividends, if any. (The returns computed here are used in other exercises.)

Correlation Matrix of Returns			
	Apple Computer	**Homestake Mining**	**FPL Group**
Apple Computer	1.0		
Homestake Mining		1.0	
FPL Group			1.0

For the two-stock portfolios shown in the table below, find the return and standard deviation of a portfolio composed of equal investment in each stock.

Portfolio Returns and Standard Deviations		
Portfolio	**Average Monthly Return**	**Standard Deviation**
Apple/Homestake		
Apple/FPL		
Homestake/FPL		

Prepare a graph showing the possible combinations of returns and standard deviations for a two-stock portfolio consisting of Apple Computer and Homestake Mining. (Let the proportion invested in Apple range from 0 to 100 percent with 1 percent increments. The remaining funds would be invested in Homestake. Let the X-axis run from .08 to .14, and set the Y-axis to run from 0 to .03.)

Exercise 54
Fixed and Adjustable Mortgage Rates

Contributed by Ricardo J. Rodriguez
Spreadsheet: MORTMKT.WK1

Prepare a graph showing the evolution of fixed and adjustable mortgage rates closed for 1982–1992. (Let the X-axis run from 1982/7 to 1992/6, and set the Y-axis to run from 6 to 17 percent.) What is the general relationship between the two rates? Why?

Exercise 55
Commercial Paper Interest Rates

Contributed by Robert W. Kolb
Spreadsheet: MONEYYLD.WK1

For January 1980 to December 1991, compute the average yield on 1-month, 3-month, and 6-month maturities of commercial paper and use these values to complete the following table.

Commercial Paper Interest Rates, 1980 to 1991		
Maturity	Mean Rate	Standard Deviation
1-month		
3-month		
6-month		

Based on the information in the table, what can you say about the typical shape of the commercial paper yield curve? Is it possible to make any concrete inference? Based on the table, what inferences are possible regarding the relative volatility of long-term versus short-term interest rates?

Exercise 56
Issuers of Commercial Paper

Contributed by Robert W. Kolb
Spreadsheet: MONEYYLD.WK1

For the period from January 1983 to December 1991, create a graph showing the total amount of commercial paper outstanding and the total amount of commercial paper outstanding that is issued by financial companies. (Let the X-axis run from 1983 to 1991, and set the Y-axis to run from 0 to 600,000.) How has this changed? Can you offer a plausible explanation for any trend you may observe?

Exercise 57
Eurodollar Yield Curves

Contributed by Robert W. Kolb
Spreadsheet: MONEYYLD.WK1

For March 1980 and March 1991, find the Eurodollar deposit rates to complete this table.

Eurodollar Deposit Rates		
Maturity	March 1980	March 1991
One–week		
One–month		
Three–month		
Six–month		
One–year		

Based on the table, what can you say about the shape of the Eurodollar yield curve on these two dates?

Exercise 58
T–Bill Auction Rates

Contributed by Robert W. Kolb
Spreadsheet: MONEYYLD.WK1

For the period January 1980 through December 1991, prepare a graph showing the average auction rates on 3-month, 6-month, and 1-year T-bill rates. (Let the X-axis run from 1980 to 1991, and set the Y-axis to run from 0 to 18.) Compute the average rates for each maturity and the corresponding standard deviation. Use these values to complete the table below. What inferences can you make from the graph and your computations about the typical relationship between rates on different maturities of T-bills?

T-bill Auction Interest Rates, 1980 to 1991		
Maturity	Mean Rate	Standard Deviation
3-month		
6-month		
1-year		

Exercise 59
Treasury Yield Curves

Contributed by Robert W. Kolb
Spreadsheets: MONEYYLD.WK1, BONDYLD.WK1

For March 1977 to December 1991, compute the difference between the yields on 30-year U.S. T-bonds and 3-month secondary market T-bills. Prepare a graph showing both yields and the difference in the yields for the period specified. (Let the X-axis run from 1977 to 1991, and set the Y-axis to run from -4 to 17.) From the graph, does the yield differential appear to be greater when yield levels are higher or lower?

Regress the yield differential (YD) on the level of T-bill yields (TB) for this period as follows:

$$YD_t = \alpha + \beta TB_t + \varepsilon_t$$

For April 1977 to December 1991, compute the change in the T-bill yield (DELTATB) and the change in the yield differential (DELTAYD). With these values perform the similar regression:

$$DELTAYD_t = \alpha + \beta DELTATB_t + \varepsilon_t$$

Specify the values for α, β, and the R^2 from the two equations below. What can you conclude from these regressions? How can you explain the differences in the results?

Regressions of Yield Differential Levels and Changes on T-Bill Rates, 1977 to 1991			
	α	β	R^2
$YD_t = \alpha + \beta TB_t + \varepsilon_t$			
$DELTAYD_t = \alpha + \beta DELTATB_t + \varepsilon_t$			

Exercise 60
Money Market Yields and the Inflation Rate

Contributed by Brian S. Wilson
Spreadsheets: INFLATE.WK1, MONEYYLD.WK1

Complete the following table depicting the correlation between the inflation rate and the yields on the various money market instruments indicated. For the inflation rate, use the monthly percentage change in the CPI. Then prepare a line graph from January 1970 through December 1991 depicting yields of each of the instruments shown in the table. For Bankers' Acceptances, use values from 1981. Which money market instrument is most highly correlated with the inflation rate? Which money market instrument is least highly correlated with the inflation rate? How does the correlation with inflation vary with the level of average yield of money market instruments?

Money Market Yields and the Inflation Rate		
Money Market Instrument	**Average Yield (1970–1991)**	**Correlation with Inflation Rate**
6-month Commercial Paper		
6-month Bankers' Acceptances		
6-month Certificates of Deposit		
6-month Eurodollar Deposit Rate		
6-month U.S. Treasury Bills		

Exercise 61
International Discount Rate Differentials

Contributed by Brian S. Wilson
Spreadsheet: FORMONEY.WK1

Complete the following table for January through December of 1988 depicting the differential present in short-term interest rates between countries. In the rate column, list the country's short-term interest rate. In the US column, subtract the country's discount rate from the Official Discount Rate of the United States. Then prepare a line graph comparing the differentials from January 1985 to December 1991.

International Discount Rate Differentials							
Period (1988)	U.S.	Germany		Japan		Switzerland	
		Rate	US	Rate	US	Rate	US
Jan							
Feb							
Mar							
Apr							
May							
Jun							
Jul							
Aug							
Sep							
Oct							
Nov							
Dec							

Which country's short-term interest rate differs most highly with that of the U.S.? Do the short-term interest rate differentials stay relatively constant?

Exercise 62
Corporate Bond Risk Differentials

Contributed by Robert W. Kolb
Spreadsheet: BONDYLD.WK1

For January 1970 to December 1991, compute the difference between the yields on AAA and BAA corporate bonds. Prepare a graph showing both yields and the difference in the yields for the period specified. (Let the X-axis run from 1970 to 1991, and set the Y-axis to run from 0 to 18.) From the graph, does the yield differential appear to be greater when yield levels are higher or lower?

Regress the yield differential (YD) on the level of AAA bond yields (AAA) for this period as follows:

$$YD_t = \alpha + \beta AAA_t + \varepsilon_t$$

For February 1970 to December 1991, compute the change in the AAA bond yield (DELTAAAA) and the change in the yield differential (DELTAYD). With these values perform the similar regression:

$$DELTAYD_t = \alpha + \beta DELTAAAA_t + \varepsilon_t$$

Specify the values for α, β, and the R^2 from the two equations below. What can you conclude from these regressions? How can you explain the differences in the results?

Regressions of Yield Differential Levels and Changes on AAA Bond Rates, 1970 to 1991			
	α	β	R^2
$YD_t = \alpha + \beta AAA_t + \varepsilon_t$			
$DELTAYD_t = \alpha + \beta DELTAAAA_t + \varepsilon_t$			

Exercise 63
Bond Market Yields and
The Inflation Rate

Contributed by Brian S. Wilson
Spreadsheets: INFLATE.WK1, BONDYLD.WK1

Complete the following table depicting the correlation between the inflation rate and the yields on the various bond market instruments indicated. For the inflation rate, use the monthly percentage change in the CPI. Then prepare a line graph from January 1970 through December 1991 depicting yields of each of the instruments shown in the table. For 10yr Municipals, use values from January 1986. Which bond market instrument is most highly correlated with the inflation rate? Which bond market instrument is least highly correlated with the inflation rate? How does the correlation with inflation vary with the level of average yield of bond market instruments? How does the correlation with inflation vary with the time remaining to maturity of the various instruments?

Bond Market Yields and the Inflation Rate		
Bond Market Instrument	**Average Yield (1970–1991)**	**Correlation with Inflation Rate**
U.S. Treasury Notes and Bonds, 3-Year Maturity		
U.S. Treasury Notes and Bonds, 10-Year Maturity		
AAA Municipal Bond Yield (20-Year)		
AAA Municipal Bond Yield (10-Year)		
AAA Corporate Bonds, Average Yield		
BAA Corporate Bonds, Average Yield		

Exercise 64
Default Risk Premium

Contributed by Brian S. Wilson
Spreadsheet: BONDYLD.WK1

Prepare a line graph depicting the yields on AAA, AA, A, and BAA corporate bonds from January 1985 through December 1990. Do the yields on the various classifications of corporate bonds imply the presence of a default risk premium? Between which two neighboring categories is this premium greatest?

Exercise 65
Default Risk Premium by Type of Bond

Contributed by Brian S. Wilson
Spreadsheet: BONDYLD.WK1

For January 1980 through July 1992, prepare a line graph displaying the average yields on AA Corporate Bonds, Long-Term Treasury Bonds, AA Industrial Bonds, and AA Utility Bonds. According to the graph, which type of bond do investors perceive as most risky? Does the relationship or spread between these average yields stay relatively constant over this period?

Exercise 66
International Government Bonds

Contributed by Robert W. Kolb
Spreadsheet: FORBOND.WK1

For the period January 1985 to December 1991, compute the mean and standard deviation of the interest rates on Australian and Japanese government treasury securities. Also, compute the monthly difference for each month and its mean and standard deviation. Use these values to complete the table shown below.

Australian and Japanese Government Bond Rates, 1985 to 1991		
Country	Average	Standard Deviation
Australia		
Japan		
Australia-Japan		

How significant is the difference in rates? How stable is the difference? What could potentially explain the difference in rates that the table reflects?

Exercise 67
Returns on Bond Portfolios

Contributed by Robert W. Kolb
Spreadsheet: FORBOND.WK1

For January 1985 to June 1992, compute the mean monthly return and standard deviation of returns for the following Salomon Brothers bond indexes: World Government, Canada, Germany, U.S., Japan, Switzerland. Use these values to complete the following table.

Government Bond Total Returns, 1985 to 1992		
Entity	**Mean**	**Standard Deviation**
World		
Canada		
Germany		
United States		
Japan		
Switzerland		

Prepare a graph in risk/return space to show these performance results. (Let the X-axis run from 0 to 2, and set the Y-axis to run from 0 to 1.2.) Which country's results were dominated for this period? Can you tell from these data? Which portfolio should have tended to dominate the others? Explain.

Compute all correlations among these indexes and use the values to complete the following correlation matrix.

Correlation of Salomon Brothers Bond Returns Indexes, 1985–1992						
	World	Canada	Germany	U.S.	Japan	Switzerland
World	1.0					
Canada		1.0				
Germany			1.0			
U.S.				1.0		
Japan					1.0	
Switzerland						1.0

For each country, which other single country offers the best prospects for diversification based on the correlation matrix? Which countries might one expect to be highly correlated with the world portfolio? Explain.

Exercise 68
Real and Nominal Returns
for World Government Bonds

Contributed by Brian S. Wilson
Spreadsheets: FORBOND.WK1, FORINFLA.WK1

Complete the following table depicting the real and nominal performance of the various foreign bond indexes. (Compute average values from January 1985 through March 1992.) Prepare a line graph depicting the real returns of the government bond indexes of France and the United Kingdom. Let the Y-axis be the real rate of return, and let the X-axis run from January 1985 to March of 1992.

Real and Nominal Returns on World Government Bond Portfolios				
Salomon Brothers World Government Bond Index	Average Monthly Nominal Return	Average Monthly Inflation Rate	Average Real Return	Standard Deviation of Real Returns
United States				
Japan				
Germany				
United Kingdom				
France				

Which index has had the highest average nominal return over the period? Which has had the highest average real return? Which country's real returns were most volatile?

Exercise 69
Currency Winners and Losers

Contributed by Robert W. Kolb
Spreadsheet: FOREX.WK1

For the period from January 1985 through December 1991, complete the following table, realizing that the values in the last row must be computed from the first two rows.

Swiss Francs, U.S. Dollars, and Brazilian Cruzeiros, 1985 to 1991			
	January 1985	December 1991	Percentage Change of First Currency Against the Second
Cruzeiros per dollar			
Swiss francs per dollar			
Cruzeiros per Swiss franc			

Exercise 70
Volatility of Exchange Rates

Contributed by Brian S. Wilson
Spreadsheet: FOREX.WK1

Complete the following table showing the volatility of exchange rates for Japan, West Germany, Mexico, and Brazil. Use standard deviation as a percent of the mean (coefficient of variation):

Volatility of Exchange Rates				
Period	Standard Deviation of Yen per U.S. Dollar (percent of mean)	Standard Deviation of Deutsche Marks per U.S. Dollar (percent of mean)	Standard Deviation of Pesos per U.S. Dollar (percent of mean)	Standard Deviation of Cruzeiros per U.S. Dollar (percent of mean)
Jan 1975 to Dec 1979				
Jan 1980 to Dec 1984				
Jan 1985 to Dec 1989				
Jan 1975 to May 1992				

In which country would an American multi-national corporation face the most currency risk? During which five-year period and in which country were exchange rates most volatile?

Exercise 71
Real and Nominal Exchange Rates

Contributed by Brian S. Wilson
Spreadsheets: FOREX.WK1, FORINFLA.WK1

Complete the following table deriving the nominal and real bilateral exchange rates between the United States and Japan with a base year of 1982. Prepare a graph that depicts the nominal and real exchange rate for each month from January 1972 to January 1992 with January 1982 values set equal to 100. Use data for January of the indicated year. The real exchange rate equals the nominal exchange rate (cents per yen) multiplied by the ratio of inflation abroad to inflation at home (CPI Japan/CPI U.S.).

	Real and Nominal Exchange Rates: U.S. and Japan						
	Nominal Exchange Rate			Real Exchange Rate			
Period	Yen per U.S.$	Cents per yen	Cents per yen (1982 = 100)	CPI Japan	CPI U.S.	Ratio: CPI Japan to CPI U.S.	Ratio (1982 = 100)
1972							
1974							
1976							
1978							
1980							
1982							
1984							
1986							
1988							
1990							
1992							

According to the graph, do the nominal and real exchange rates correlate highly? What does a rise in the real exchange rate imply?

Exercise 72
Volatile Exchange Rates

Contributed by Brian S. Wilson
Spreadsheet: FOREX.WK1

Complete the following table depicting the coefficients of variation of the exchange rates shown. Prepare a graph running from March of 1974 through July of 1992 of the exchange rate of South Africa. For Argentina, begin in January of 1976.

	Highly Volatile Exchange Rates		
	Cruzeiros per U.S.$	Cents per Rand	Australes per U.S.$
Period	Standard Deviation (% of mean)	Standard Deviation (% of mean)	Standard Deviation (% of mean)
1-74 to 12-79			
1-80 to 12-84			
1-85 to 12-89			
1-74 to 12-91			

Which exchange rate was most volatile from 1974 through 1991?

Exercise 73
Correlations Among Stock Indexes and Business Cycle Indexes

Contributed by Brian S. Wilson
Spreadsheets: STKINDEX.WK1, BUSCYCLE.WK1

Convert the Dow Jones Industrial Average to a base in which June of 1982 = 100. Use these converted values to complete the correlation matrix below containing the Composite Index of 4 Coincident Indicators (BC016), the Composite Index of 7 Lagging Indicators (BC021), and the Composite Index of 11 Leading Indicators.

Correlation Matrix for Stock and Business Cycle Indexes	
Business Cycle Index:	**Correlation With DJIA (June 1982 = 100):**
Leading Index	
Lagging Index	
Coincident Index	

Based on the completed table, with which index does the Dow Jones Industrial Average have the highest correlation? As what kind of indicator, then, would you say the Dow Jones Industrial Average functions?

Exercise 74
The Predictive Capabilities of the
Composite Index of Leading Indicators

Contributed by Brian S. Wilson
Spreadsheets: NATLPROD.WK1, BUSCYCLE.WK1, FINQU.WK1

Prepare a line graph that compares Total Gross Domestic Product to The Composite Index of 11 Leading Indicators. In order to compare the two series, use Leading Index values for March, June, September, and December for each year beginning in March 1970 and ending in December 1991. Also, convert Total Gross Domestic Product so that March of 1982 = 100. Then adjust Total Gross Domestic Product for inflation. Use Total Gross Domestic Product values beginning in the first quarter of 1970 and ending in the fourth quarter of 1991.

Prepare a second line graph similar to the first, except lag the Total Gross Domestic Product series one quarter; that is, begin in the second quarter of 1970 and end in the first quarter of 1992.

Prepare a third line graph similar to the first, except lag the Total Gross Domestic Product series two quarters; that is, begin in the third quarter of 1970 and end in the second quarter of 1992.

According to the graph, does the Composite Index of Leading Indicators appear to be correlated with the level of Gross Domestic Product? Does the Composite Index of Leading Indicators serve as a useful predictor of the general trend of Gross Domestic Product?

Total Gross Domestic Product Conversion: ((value x/3-92 value)*100
Adjustment for inflation: (converted value)*(CPI/100)

Exercise 75
Volatility of The Components of GNP

Contributed by Brian S. Wilson
Spreadsheet: NATLPROD.WK1

Complete the following table showing the respective means and coefficients of variation of the various components of GNP. Give the standard deviation as a percent of the mean.

	Volatility of the Components of GNP							
Period	**Consumption**		**Investment**		**Government Purchases**		**Net Exports**	
	Mean	**Std. Dev.**	**Mean**	**Std. Dev.**	**Mean**	**Std. Dev.**	**Mean**	**Std. Dev.**
Q1 1970–Q4 1974								
Q1 1975–Q4 1979								
Q1 1980–Q4 1984								
Q1 1985–Q4 1990								

Based on your calculations, and a visual analysis of the table, which component of GNP is most erratic? During which period was GNP most volatile?

Exercise 76
Real GNP and Nominal GNP

Contributed by Brian S. Wilson
Spreadsheets: NATLPROD.WK1, FINQU.WK1

For the period of Quarter 2 of 1970 through Quarter 2 of 1992, create a line graph comparing the monthly percent change in real GNP (derive real GNP by using the GNP deflator, the GNP deflator is the ratio of nominal GNP to real GNP) and the monthly percent change in nominal GNP. Based on the graph, do you notice any periods where the percent change in real GNP is negative and the percent change in nominal GNP is positive? How can you categorize such a period?

Exercise 77
Components of GNP:
The Expenditure Approach

Contributed by Brian S. Wilson
Spreadsheet: NATLPROD.WK1

Complete the following table and create a stacked-bar graph composed of the following GNP components according to the expenditure approach.

	Components of GNP: The Expenditure Approach			
Year	Consumption (% of Total)	Investment (% of Total)	Government Purchases (% of Total)	Net Exports (% of Total)
1950				
1960				
1970				
1980				
1990				

How has the relationship between these components changed over time?

Exercise 78
Components of Investment Spending

Contributed by Brian S. Wilson
Spreadsheet: NATLPROD.WK1

Prepare a graph, from Quarter 1 of 1950 through Quarter 2 of 1992, depicting the following investment components as a percentage of GNP: Total Gross Private Domestic Investment, Non-residential Fixed Investment, Residential Fixed Investment, and Total Change in Business Inventories. During which decade has investment fallen the most as a percentage of GNP? During which decade was Total Gross Private Domestic Investment the highest as a percentage of GNP? Why is investment always a focal point when analyzing business cycles?

Exercise 79
Government Purchases
and Gross Domestic Product

Contributed by Robert W. Kolb
Spreadsheets: NATLPROD.WK1

Prepare a graph that shows total seasonally adjusted government purchases of goods and services as a percentage of total seasonally adjusted gross domestic product for 1959–1989. (Let the X-axis run from 1959 to 1989, and set the Y-axis to run from .16 to .22.)

Compute the mean of this percentage for the 1960s, 1970s, and 1980s and complete the following table.

Decade	Mean Ratio of Total Government Purchases of Goods and Services to Total Gross Domestic Product
1960s	
1970s	
1980s	

How has this relationship changed over time? The 1980s have the reputation of being a period of large tax cuts. Were these tax cuts accompanied by a relative decrease in government spending?

Exercise 80
Gross Domestic Product and Consumption

Contributed by Robert W. Kolb
Spreadsheet: NATLPROD.WK1

Prepare a graph that shows total personal consumption expenditures as a percentage of total seasonally adjusted gross domestic product for 1959–1989. (Let the X-axis run from 1959 to 1989, and set the Y-axis to run from .6 to .7.)

Compute the mean of this percentage for the 1960s, 1970s, and 1980s and complete the table shown below.

Decade	Mean Ratio of Total Personal Consumption to Total Gross Domestic Product
1960s	
1970s	
1980s	

How has this relationship changed over time? The 1980s have the reputation of being a time of extreme consumption and self-indulgence. Do these statistics support the view that the 1980s were different from previous periods?

Exercise 81
National Income and Its Distribution

Contributed by Brian S. Wilson
Spreadsheet: NATLPROD.WK1

Complete the table below using data from the second quarter of the year listed. (Dollar amounts are in billions). How has the distribution of national income changed over time? How has the distribution of national income among proprietors and corporations changed since 1950?

	National Income and Its Distribution							
	Compensation of Employees		Proprietor Income		Rental Income		Corporate Profits	
Year	$	%	$	%	$	%	$	%
1950								
1960								
1970								
1980								
1990								

Exercise 82
The Personal Saving Rate

Contributed by Brian S. Wilson
Spreadsheet: PERINCOM.WK1

For the period from the first quarter of 1960 through the fourth quarter of 1991, prepare a line graph showing personal saving as a percent of personal disposable income. Did the tax cuts throughout the 1980s increase personal saving relative to personal disposable income?

Exercise 83
Real Personal Income

Contributed by Brian S. Wilson
Spreadsheets: FINQU.WK1, PERINCOM.WK1

Complete the table below by calculating the values for the descriptions given in the appropriate spreadsheets. For Average Personal Income for 1950, compute the average of the values for quarters one through four.

The purchasing power of your real income is defined as current income adjusted for inflation according to the formula: Y(real) = Y(current)/(CPI/100). To complete the third column, compute real personal income in 1983 dollars for each year.

Real Personal Income			
Year	Average Personal Income (billions of Dollars)	Average CPI: All Items (1982–1984 = 100)	Real Personal Income (1983 dollars)
1950			
1960			
1970			
1980			
1990			

Exercise 84
Personal Consumption Expenditures

Contributed by Brian S. Wilson
Spreadsheet: PERINCOM.WK1

Complete the following table using second quarter data:

Personal Consumption Expenditures				
Year	Personal Consumption Expenditures: Total	Personal Consumption Expenditures: Durable Goods (% of Total)	Personal Consumption Expenditures: Nondurable Goods (% of Total)	Personal Consumption Expenditures: Services (% of Total)
1946				
1950				
1955				
1960				
1965				
1970				
1975				
1980				
1985				
1990				

Based on a visual inspection of the table do you think that the U.S. economy is becoming increasingly service-oriented?

Exercise 85
Personal Consumption Expenditures:
By Component

Contributed by Brian S. Wilson
Spreadsheet: PERINCOM.WK1

Complete the following table depicting the Components of Personal Consumption Expenditures as a percent of total during the period indicated. For electricity, use 1959, and for Medical Care, use 1947, instead of 1946.

Personal Consumption Expenditures: By Component				
Component	Q2, 1946	Average Q1 1981 to Q4 1983 (recession)	Average Q1 1984 to Q4 1986 (recovery)	Q2, 1992
Durable Goods				
Nondurable Goods				
Services				
Food				
Clothing and Shoes				
Gas and Oil				
Housing				
Electricity				
Transportation				
Medical Care				

How have personal consumption expenditures changed since 1946? Is there a noticeable difference in consumption behavior during a recession or recovery?

Exercise 86
Growth in Real GNP and
The Employment Rate

Contributed by Brian S. Wilson
Spreadsheets: EMPLOY.WK1, NATLPROD.WK1, FINQU.WK1

Prepare a scatter diagram comparing the average quarterly percentage change in real GNP and the average quarterly change in the employment rate for each year from 1971 through 1991. For the first quarter of each year, compute the percentage change from the fourth quarter of the prior year. Use the CPI from the FINQU.WK1 spreadsheet to compute real GNP. Set the Y-axis as the average quarterly growth rate of real GNP and set the X-axis as increase in employment rates (percentage points). Use the employment rate for March, June, September, and December to correspond to quarterly GNP. How do high and low rates of growth affect the employment rate?

Exercise 87
The Changing Labor Force

Contributed by Brian S. Wilson
Spreadsheet: EMPLOY.WK1

Prepare a bar graph showing the number of men employed as a percent of total, and the number of women employed as a percent of total for December of each year running from 1970 through 1990. (Set the X axis to run from 1970 to 1990. Set the Y-axis to run from 0% to 70%.) Does the graph you created give merit to the theory that more and more women are entering the work force?

Exercise 88
Corporate Tax Revenue and Employment

Contributed by Brian S. Wilson
Spreadsheets: FEDFISCL.WK1, EMPLOY.WK1, FINQU.WK1

Prepare two line graphs that illustrate Inflation Adjusted Corporate Tax Revenue and the Employment Rate from Quarter 1 1970 to Quarter 4 1990. For the Employment Rate use values from March, June, September, and December. (Let the X-axis for both graphs run from Quarter 1 1970 to Quarter 4 1990, and set the Y-axes to run from 40 to 120 for Corporate Tax Revenue and 89 to 97 for the Employment Rate. Do these series seem highly correlated? What could be the explanation for the correlation between these two factors? Hint: Define the inflation adjusted corporate tax revenue as [FIS004/(FINQU005/100)], and let the Employment Rate equal (100 - Unemployment Rate).

Exercise 89
The Discomfort Index

Contributed by Brian S. Wilson
Spreadsheets: EMPLOY.WK1, INFLATE.WK1

The Discomfort Index equals the inflation rate plus the overall unemployment rate. Complete the following table showing the discomfort index for the periods listed below. For the inflation rate, use the average annual percentage change in the CPI over the period, and for unemployment, use the average monthly unemployment rate for the period.

The Discomfort Index			
Period	Average Inflation Rate	Average Unemployment Rate	Discomfort Index
Jan 1970–Dec 1974			
Jan 1975–Dec 1979			
Jan 1980–Dec 1984			
Jan 1985–Dec 1989			

During which period was the Discomfort Index the highest? What is the Discomfort Index for December 1990?

Exercise 90
Construction, Production, and the Employment Rate

Contributed by Brian S. Wilson
Spreadsheets: INDUPROD.WK1, HOUSING.WK1, EMPLOY.WK1

Complete the following correlation matrix using values from January 1970 to March of 1992. For the employment rate, use one minus the unemployment rate setting the June of 1987 value equal to 100. Then prepare a line graph comparing the three indexes. Set the Y-axis equal to the respective index values, and the X-axis to run from January 1970 to March 1992.

Correlation Matrix for Construction, Production, and Employment			
	Construction Index: Composite Fixed-Weight Price Index (1987 = 100)	Industrial Production Index: Total Index (1987 = 100)	Employment Rate Index (1987 = 100)
Construction Index: Composite Fixed-Weight Price Index (1987 = 100)	1.0		
Industrial Production Index: Total Index (1987 = 100)		1.0	
Employment Rate Index (1987 = 100)			1.0

Is there any correlation between industrial production and construction? Is production or construction more correlated with the employment rate?

Exercise 91
Real Cost of Employment and
Real Total Gross Domestic Product

Contributed by Brian S. Wilson
Spreadsheets: WAGES.WK1, NATLPROD.WK1, FINQU.WK1

Complete the following table depicting the average monthly cost of employment indexes and real Gross Domestic Product since 1976. As a measure of the cost of employment, use the employment cost index of the wages and salaries of all private non-farm workers. Use the CPI from the FINQU.WK1 spreadsheet to adjust each for inflation. Then prepare a graph depicting the Real Cost of Employment and Real Total Gross Domestic Product. For the graph, set the Q2 1989 value of Total Real GDP equal to 100, extend to Q2 1992.

Real Cost of Employment and Real Gross Domestic Product					
Period	Avg. Percent Change in CPI Index	Avg. Percent Change in Nominal Cost of Employment Index	Avg. Percent Change in Nominal Gross Domestic Product	Avg. Percent Change in Real Cost of Employment Index	Avg. Percent Change in Real Gross Domestic Product
Q1 1976 to Q4 1979					
Q1 1980 to Q4 1984					
Q1 1985 to Q4 1989					

How have the cost of employment changes compared with changes in inflation? Have employees become more efficient based on changes in Gross Domestic Product?

Exercise 92
Changes in Real Wages

Contributed by Brian S. Wilson
Spreadsheets: WAGES.WK1, FINQU.WK1

Complete the following table comparing the percentage change in the nominal wages and salaries of White-Collar Workers, Blue-Collar Workers, and Union Workers with the percentage change in the Consumer Price Index. Also, prepare a line graph, running from the first quarter of 1976 through the first quarter of 1992, of the Indexes of the Wages and Salaries of White-Collar Workers, Blue-Collar Workers, and Union Workers adjusted for inflation. To convert the indexes to real values, divide the respective index by the CPI/100. Set the Y-axis equal to the various indexes, and set the X-axis to run from the first quarter of 1976 through the second quarter of 1992.

Changes in Real Wages				
Period	Avg. Percent Increase in Wages of White-Collar Workers	Avg. Percent Increase in Wages of Blue-Collar Workers	Avg. Percent Increase in Wages of Union Workers	Avg. Percent Increase in Consumer Price Index
Q1 1976 to Q4 1979				
Q1 1980 to Q4 1984				
Q1 1985 to Q2 1992				
Q1 1976 to Q2 1992				

Do increases in wages and salaries seem to correspond to increases in inflation? Which type of worker has seen the largest wage increases from 1976 to 1992? Compare the behavior of real wages in general by type of worker from 1976 to 1992.

Exercise 93
Federal Government:
Receipts and Expenditures

Contributed by Brian S. Wilson
Spreadsheet: FEDFISCL.WK1

Create a line graph of the ratio of Federal government expenditures to Federal government receipts. Set the X-axis to be every other year from 1950 to 1992. Let the Y-axis values be the average quarterly ratio of expenditures to receipts for the respective year. Then complete the following table:

Federal Government: Receipts and Expenditures				
Period	Average Receipts	Average Expenditures	Ratio of Average Expenditures to Average Receipts	% Change from 1950
1950				
1960				
1970				
1980				
1990				

How has this ratio changed over time? Do you think this ratio can be maintained throughout the 21st century?

Exercise 94
The Composition of Federal Outlays

Contributed by Brian S. Wilson
Spreadsheet: FEDFISCL.WK1

Prepare a line graph from the first quarter of 1950 to the fourth quarter of 1991 depicting Purchases of Goods and Services–Nondefense, National Defense, Net Transfer Payments, Grants-In-Aid to State and Local Governments, and Total Interest Paid, as a percentage of total expenditures. Complete the table below using first quarter data of the indicated year, showing components of expenditures as a percent of total expenditures.

The Composition of Federal Outlays					
Year	National Defense	Nondefense	Transfer Payments	Grants-In-Aid	Net Interest Paid
1950					
1960					
1970					
1980					
1990					

Which components of Federal expenditures increased relative to the others from 1950 to 1990? According to the graph, which component of Federal Government expenditures has shown the most variance as a percent of total?

Exercise 95
Federal Government: Net Interest Paid

Contributed by Brian S. Wilson
Spreadsheet: FEDFISCL.WK1

Using first quarter data, prepare a stacked-bar graph of the relationship between Federal Government Expenditures and Net Interest Paid by the Federal Government based on values that you compute to complete the following table:

	Federal Government: Net Interest Paid		
Year	Federal Government: Expenditures, Total	Federal Government: Expenditures, Net Interest Paid	Net Interest Paid as a % of Total Expenditures
1960			
1970			
1980			
1990			

Has this relationship changed over time? How does Net Interest Paid in the first quarter of 1990 compare with Total Expenditures in 1950?

Exercise 96
The Budget Deficit and Real Interest Rates

Contributed by Brian S. Wilson
Spreadsheets: FINQU.WK1, FEDFISCL.WK1, NATLPROD.WK1

For the period from 1972 to 1990, create a graph depicting the real interest rate and the budget deficit as a percentage of GNP. The real interest rate is defined as the nominal interest rate minus the percentage rate of inflation. To complete your line graph, use the values you derive in the following table:

The Budget Deficit and Real Interest Rates						
Year	Deficit	GNP	Deficit as % of GNP	Nominal Interest Rate	% Change in Inflation	Real Interest Rate
1972						
1974						
1976						
1978						
1980						
1982						
1984						
1986						
1988						
1990						

What relationship do you observe between the deficit and real interest rates?

Exercise 97
The Budget Deficit and The Trade Deficit

Contributed by Brian S. Wilson
Spreadsheets: FEDFISCL.WK1, NATLPROD.WK1

Prepare a line graph comparing the deficit to the trade balance from the first quarter of 1960 through the fourth quarter of 1989. Do you see a high correlation between these two series? What could this correlation be attributed to?

Exercise 98
The Correlation Between Sales and Output

Contributed by Brian S. Wilson
Spreadsheets: MANUFAC.WK1, NATLPROD.WK1, FINQU.WK1

Prepare a graph depicting inflation adjusted (real) Manufacturing and Trade Sales, Retail Trade, and GNP for the first quarter of 1970 through the second quarter of 1991. Adjust both series so that the first quarter of 1982 = 100. For sales data use the months March, June, September, and December. Use the CPI in the spreadsheet FINQU.WK1 to adjust GNP for inflation. According to the graph, do sales and output seem correlated? Using the values contained in the graph for the two series (1982 = 100), compute the correlation coefficient between the two variables.

Exercise 99
U.S. and Foreign Automobiles: Expenditures and Sales

Contributed by Brian S. Wilson
Spreadsheet: AUTOS.WK1

Prepare a line graph comparing retail automobile and truck sales of domestic and foreign new passenger cars from January 1970 to June 1992. Prepare another line graph comparing the average expenditure per car over the same period, and complete the following table using average monthly statistics:

	U.S. and Foreign Automobiles: Expenditures and Sales					
	Domestic Automobiles			Foreign Automobiles		
Year	Average Expenditure	Sales	Corr.	Average Expenditure	Sales	Corr.
1970						
1975						
1980						
1985						
1990						

How has the relationship between foreign and domestic automobiles sold changed over time? Have U.S. expenditures per automobile been historically higher than foreign expenditures per automobile?

Exercise 100
Inventory-to-Sales Ratio
of the Automotive Industry

Contributed by Brian S. Wilson
Spreadsheets: AUTOS.WK1, MANUFAC.WK1

Complete the following table comparing the inventory-to-sales ratio of the automotive industry in comparison with the aggregate inventory-to-sales ratio of all retail trade. Prepare a line graph comparing the two ratios. Set the X-axis from January 1970 through December 1990, and let the Y-axis equal the inventory to sales ratio.

Inventory–to–Sales Ratio of the Automotive Industry		
Period	Average Inventory to Sales Ratio: Retail Trade	Average Inventory to Sales Ratio: Automotive Dealers
Jan 70 to Dec 74		
Jan 75 to Dec 79		
Jan 80 to Dec 84		
Jan 85 to Dec 89		
Jan 90 to Dec 90		
Jan 70 to Dec 90		

On average, do automotive dealers hold more inventory than retailers as a whole? Is the inventory to sales ratio of automotive dealers more volatile? Has the amount of inventory held by automotive dealers or aggregate retailers changed over time?

Exercise 101
Corporate Profits by Industrial Sector

Contributed by Brian S. Wilson
Spreadsheets: CORPPROF.WK1, FINQU.WK1

Complete the following table depicting the mean and coefficient of variation of nominal and real quarterly corporate profits of the various industrial sectors shown from Q1 of 1947 through Q4 of 1991. The coefficient of variation is standard deviation as a percent of the mean. Prepare two line graphs, from Q1 1947 through Q4 1991, the first comparing the real quarterly corporate profits of construction and financial institutions, the second depicting the quarterly percent change in nominal profits of mining and public utilities.

Corporate Profits by Industrial Sector				
Industrial Sector	Mean Nominal Quarterly Corporate Profits	Coefficient of Variation of Nominal Quarterly Corporate Profits	Mean Quarterly Real Corporate Profits	Coefficient of Variation of Real Quarterly Corporate Profits
Financial Institutions				
Manufacturing				
Public Utilities				
Wholesale and Retail Trade				
Mining				
Construction				
Transportation				
Communication				
Finance, etc.				
Services				

Which sector has shown the highest profit volatility? Compare the evolution of financial institutions and construction. Compare the volatility of mining and manufacturing.

Exercise 102
The Aggregate Inventory-to-Sales Ratio

Contributed by Brian S. Wilson
Spreadsheet: MANUFAC.WK1

Prepare a line graph running from January 1970 through June 1992 depicting the ratio of inventories (book value) to sales. Then complete the table below.

The Aggregate Inventory–to–Sales Ratio	
Period	**Average Ratio of Inventories (Book Value) to Sales**
January 1970–December 1974	
January 1975–December 1979	
January 1980–December 1984	
January 1985–December 1989	
January 1990–June 1992	

How has this relationship changed over time? What does a high inventory-to-sales ratio imply?

Exercise 103
Inventory as an Economic Indicator

Contributed by Brian S. Wilson
Spreadsheets: MANUFAC.WK1, BUSCYCLE.WK1

Prepare a line graph from January 1970 through August 1991 depicting the inventory-to-sales ratios of manufacturers, merchant wholesalers, and retailers. Then complete the following table:

Inventory as an Economic Indicator			
Definition of Inventory	**Correlation with Composite Index of Leading Indicators**	**Correlation with Composite Index of Lagging Indicators**	**Correlation With Coincident Indicators**
Manufacturing Inventories			
Inventories of Merchant Wholesalers			
Retail Trade Inventories			

Discuss the correlations you computed to complete the table and the value of the varying definitions of inventory as an indicator of economic activity. How do inventory-to-sales ratios vary by the component of the vertical chain of sales?

Exercise 104
An Industrial Energy Efficiency Index

Contributed by Ricardo J. Rodriguez
Spreadsheets: ENERGY.WK1, INDUPROD.WK1

Prepare a graph showing the evolution of the ratio of total energy consumption to the total index of industrial production for 1974–1992. (Let the X-axis run from 1974/1 to 1992/4, and set the Y-axis to run from 0.05 to 0.11.) Notice that the index is only useful as a relative measure of energy usage. Thus, a downward trend would indicate that U.S. industry is more efficient in using energy. Notice also, that energy is used by other sectors of the economy, e.g., households, so this index captures more than industrial utilization.

Based on the graph, what noteworthy patterns are apparent? Is the U.S. using its energy more efficiently now than in the recent past?

Exercise 105
Per Capita Energy Consumption

Contributed by Ricardo J. Rodriguez
Spreadsheets: ENERGY.WK1, EMPLOY.WK1

Prepare a graph showing the evolution of the ratio of total energy consumption to the total population of people 16 years and over for 1974–1992. (Let the X-axis run from 1974/1 to 1992/4, and set the Y-axis to run from 25 to 55 million BTUs per capita per year.)

Based on the graph, what noteworthy patterns are apparent? Is the U.S. population using its energy more efficiently now than in the recent past? Compute the average per capita energy usage and complete the table shown below.

Per Capita Energy Consumption in the United States (million BTUs per year)		
Period	**Average**	**Standard Deviation**
1974–1979		
1980–1989		
1974–1992		

Exercise 106
The Nominal and Real Price of Gasoline

Contributed by Ricardo J. Rodriguez
Spreadsheets: ENERGY.WK1, INFLATE.WK1

Prepare a graph showing the evolution of the nominal and real prices of gasoline in U.S. cities at the retail level for 1978–1992. Use the consumer price index for all items to deflate nominal gas prices. (Let the X-axis run from 1978/1 to 1992/7, and set the Y-axis to run from 40 to 160 cents.)

What noteworthy characteristics are apparent in the graph?

Exercise 107
The Value of the Dollar and the Trade Balance With Germany and Japan

Contributed by Brian S. Wilson
Spreadsheet: FOREX.WK1, TRADEBAL.WK1

Complete the following table depicting the U.S. trade balance with Germany and Japan and the bilateral exchange rate of the U.S. dollar and the respective foreign currency. Prepare two line graphs, the first depicting the trade balance with Japan and the number of yen per dollar. Set the June of 1982 value for each series equal to 100. For the second graph, do the same for Germany. Set the X-axes to run from January 1975 through June 1992.

Period	Avg. U.S.-Japan Trade Balance	Avg. Yen per U.S. Dollar	Correlation Coefficient	Avg. U.S.-Germany Trade Balance	Avg. DM per U.S. Dollar	Correlation Coefficient
The Value of the Dollar and the Trade Balance with Germany and Japan						
Jan 1975-Dec 1979						
Jan 1980-Dec 1984						
Jan 1985-Dec 1989						
Jan 1990-Jun 1992						

In general, are the respective exchange rates and the respective trade balances correlated? Describe the general trend of the trade balances between the United States and Germany and Japan since 1975.

Global Corporate Finance: Text and Cases—Second Edition

Suk H. Kim and Seung H. Kim

Chapter Outline

I. Introduction

II. International Monetary Environment

III. Financing International Transaction

IV. Asset Management

V. Reporting and Controlling

VI. Case Problems In International Corporate Finance

Text Features...

Global Corporate Finance: Text and Cases, Second Edition is designed to provide all the basic tools and techniques of international financial analysis without an overly complex treatment of theoretical financial concepts. Kim and Kim use a clear, readable, and practical case-study approach aimed at instructors with a "hands-on" orientation who want their students to possess practical, job-oriented international finance skills. The text covers all areas of international finance in sufficient detail to focus students on the truly important issues.

Global Corporate Finance: Text and Cases, Second Edition contains several special features including:

- Up-to-date coverage of the European monetary crisis.
- Case-studies based on actual situations and real firms illustrate major points including: U.S. Steel Imports, Trade Friction Between the U.S. and Korea, A North American Free Trade Area, The Columbian Peso, Olivetti's Exposure, Who Is Number 1: the U.S. or Japan?, LSI Logic Corp., NUMMI, Ford disinvestment in South Africa, World Electronic Corporation and Advanced Technology Company.
- End-of chapter problems tied to numerical examples presented in each chapter.
- 400 key terms contained in a quick reference glossary
- **Skeleton** and **STUDY!** software, along with a **Student Resource Manual** including software instructions, and an **Instructor's Package** that contains a complete set of ancillary materials chapter theme, chapter outline, answers to end-of-chapter questions, solutions to end-of chapter problems, a test bank of 400 multiple choice questions, transparency masters for key tables and figures, and complete lecture outlines. (*see pages 10 and 11 for more details!*)

Financial Institutions and Markets

Robert W. Kolb and Ricardo J. Rodriguez

Chapter Outline

Text Features...

Financial Institutions and Markets provides a thorough introduction to the financial system of the United States and includes a substantial international focus as well. The text is equally suitable for a first course in finance or in a course that follows an introductory corporate finance class.

Financial Institutions and Markets has many special features that distinguish it from its competitors. The text:

- Breaks the non-analytical tradition—For example: Chapters 4 and 5 provide a detailed two-chapter treatment of the time value of money.
- Offers a more analytic approach to duration, to equity valuation, to cash management, to the Black-Scholes option pricing model, all of which are presented, discussed, and illustrated numerically.
- Provides unparalleled coverage of derivatives, including separate chapters on futures, options, swaps, and financial engineering.
- Discusses the Pension Benefit Guaranty Corporation and relates its financial troubles to those that have plagued depository institutions.
- Details asset and liability management.
- Features separate chapters on finance and insurance companies.
- Includes **RealData**, a collection of historical data series covering a wide range of financial institutions and markets. The Software Instruction Manual includes many exercises that students can complete using **RealData** data.
- **Skeleton, STUDY!, RealData,** and **Spreadsheet Models for Financial Institutions** software, along with a **Student Resource Manual,** a **Software Instruction Manual**, and an **Instructor's Package**. (*see pages 10 and 11 for details!*)

Introduction to Investments

Rosemary Thomas Cunningham and Robert W. Kolb

Chapter Outline

Text Features...

Introduction to Investments is intended for a student's first course in investments and or securities analysis. Recognizing that this may be the only course a student takes in the field, the text surveys the standard topics in the investments field by investigating the primary assets available in the financial markets. It presents the information in a variety of formats that are sure to maximize a student's understanding of the material.

Introduction to Investments contains a number of special features including:

- Coverage of stock, bond, futures, and options markets, as well as mutual funds, real estate, and international investing.
- Discussions of economic activity and investments.
- Explanations of the role of the Federal Reserve in influencing interest rates and economic activity.
- Three chapters on economics, providing the necessary foundation for an understanding of investments.
- "Real world" examples of chapter topics, taken from the national and international press.
- Simplified mathematical treatment of issues, even for advanced topics such as the Black-Scholes option pricing model.
- Step-by-step detailing of all mathematical applications
- Coverage of the international dimension of securities investments.
- Concise, comprehensive definitions of key terms.
- **Skeleton, STUDY!, Investmaster,** and **Spreadsheet Models for Investments** software, along with a **Student Resource Manual,** a **Software Instruction Manual,** and an **Instructor's Package.** (*see pages 10 and 11 for details!*)

Investments, Third Edition
Robert W. Kolb

Chapter Outline

I. Market Fundamentals and Organization

II. Investing in Fixed Income Obligations

III. Investing in Equities

IV. Portfolio Management

V. Financial Derivatives and Risk Management

Expanded Coverage

The third edition of *Investments* has been thoroughly updated and edited for maximum comprehension. *Investments* contains numerical examples to clarify quantitative subject matter, and it is written in a manner that is accessible to your students. Students can easily use the text in conjunction with the ancillary materials to master topics that are not covered in class.

Investments, Third Edition contains a number of features and improvements, including:

- Expanded coverage of institutional features of the market.
- Coverage of convexity for bonds.
- Completely new chapter on swaps.
- All new chapter on financial engineering.
- Coverage of mean reversion and noise trading.
- An analysis of American Depositary Receipts.
- Coverage of the underpricing of IPOs.
- A discussion of dedicated portfolios and contingent immunization.
- Each chapter contains a "Finance Today" section for practical insight into contemporary investments. Topics covered include: Calculating Corporate Tax Rates; Foreign Companies and U.S. Taxes; Credit Rating Agencies; LDC Debt Rescheduling; Portfolio Theory; Professors Trading in the Stock Market; GLOBEX; Municipal and LYONs.
- The "International Perspectives" features add a global dimension to each chapter. Topics covered include: Japanese Zero Coupon Bonds; Assessing Country Risk; The European Currency Unit; P-E Ratios in the United States and Japan; The Big Mac Index and more!
- **Skeleton, STUDY!, Investmaster,** and **Spreadsheet Models for Investments** software, along with a **Student Resource Manual,** a **Software Instruction Manual,** and an **Instructor's Package.** (*see pages 10 and 11 for details!*)

Included In All Four Packages:

Student Resource Manual

This unique manual goes a step beyond the conventional study guide. For each chapter, the manual provides learning objectives and a detailed outline. Every chapter has a multiple–choice self–test, along with study problems (with solutions) where appropriate.

Software Instruction Manual

This user–friendly guide describes each piece of software and its operation. The complete instructions allow students to familiarize themselves with the software on their own time and at their own pace. The Software Instruction Manual addresses each program separately. It provides needed information on what a program does; installation; operation; exit procedures, and report generation. By having a book-length set of instructions, students can be confident that they can use the software without difficulty.(Note: The Software Manual for *Global Corporate Finance: Text and Cases, 2/E* is included in the Student Resource Manual.)

Instructor's Package

In addition to the text, software, Student Resource Manual and Software Instruction Manual, each text has an Instructor's Package that includes:

- Answers and solutions to all end–of–chapter questions and problems
- A printed multiple–choice test bank
- A computerized version of the test bank
- Transparency masters of key tables and figures
- Transparency masters of complete lecture outlines

Value Pricing

The wholesale price of each package is $45. While each bookstore determines its own retail price, the price to the student should be $58–60. This is comparable to the price of most unaccompanied texts, but our packages include a text, Student Resource Manual, Software Instruction Manual, and software.

Software

Each text-package contains at least two pieces of useful teaching software.

Skeleton

Written specifically for each text-package, Skeleton is an outlining program for the entire text. Skeleton is designed to reveal the underlying logical structure of the book. Skeleton features colorful, overlapping boxes that develop on–screen as the student explores each chapter.

STUDY!

Essentially, this program is itself a study guide on a disk designed individually for each package. STUDY! allows the student to select any combination of chapters to study, and the program then loads a random sequence of multiple–choice questions and presents them to the student. The program evaluates the student's answers and keeps a running score on the screen as well.

Spreadsheet Models

Richard Followill of Appalachian State University has created approximately 20 spreadsheet models that run under Lotus 123 or any compatible spreadsheet program. The spreadsheets cover the entire range of investment and financial institution topics.

Investmaster

Investmaster includes ten modules covering the most important investments topics, such as the time value of money, portfolio analysis, and the Black–Scholes option pricing model. Many modules allow the student to graph the relationships among variables. Investmaster is easy to use, with all data and answers appearing directly on screen. The program stores and retrieves data, graphs, and saves graphs to disk for printing with most popular word processing programs.

RealData

RealData includes actual historical data contained in easy-to-use spreadsheet files. All data files can be used by all major spreadsheet products including Lotus 123, Quattro Pro, Excel, and many others. RealData features data on federal taxation and expenditures, national income and product accounts, wages, the Federal Reserve, stock prices, interest rates, stock indexes, mutual funds **and more!**
PLEASE REFER TO SPECIFIC BOOK PAGES FOR THE SOFTWARE INCLUDED IN EACH TEXT-PACKAGE.

ORDER FORM

To receive your copy of any of our text-packages, please complete the form below, correct your address if necessary, and mail or fax this page to us.

Yes, I would like to consider the following for a course I teach or expect to teach in the next year.

Title:	
Course:	
Title:	
Course:	

KK **Kolb Publishing Company**
KOLB 4705 S.W. 72nd Avenue
Miami, Florida 33155

BULK RATE
U.S. POSTAGE
PAID
PERMIT NO.
03472
MIAMI, FL

Frederic L. Pryor
Professor
Swarthmore College
Swarthmore, PA 19081